Lake District
Western Fells

Dalesman Publishing Company
The Water Mill, Broughton Hall,
Skipton, North Yorkshire BD23 3AG

First Edition 1999
Reprinted 2005

Text © Paddy Dillon 1999
Maps by Jeremy Ashcroft
Cover photograph: Borrowdale by David Tarn

A British Library Cataloguing-in-Publication
record is available for this book

ISBN 185568 122 6

Printed in China

Lake District

Western Fells

Paddy Dillon

**Companion volume to
Lake District Eastern Fells**

Series editor Terry Marsh

Dalesman

Western Fells

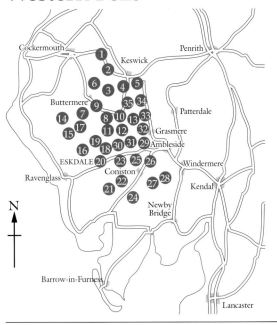

Cockermouth
Keswick
Penrith
Buttermere
Patterdale
Grasmere
Ambleside
Windermere
ESKDALE
Coniston
Ravenglass
Kendal
Newby
Bridge

N

Barrow-in-Furness

Lancaster

Contents

INTRODUCTION

All the walks in this book lie to the west of a line that runs from Bassenthwaite Lake, through Keswick, past Thirlmere, over Dunmail Raise, past Grasmere to Ambleside, and finally along the length of Windermere. The walks are immensely varied, from high fells to lake shores. There are mountain walks, hill walks, moorland walks, forest walks, riverside walks, and walks which pass through fields, villages and towns. Together they offer an insight into the landscape of the Lake District, its life, work and traditions.

Geology

The ancient Ordovician bedrocks of the Lake District are the Skiddaw Slates, which form the friable screes covering much of the northern and north-western fells, as well as the area around Black Combe in the south. Most of the central parts of Lakeland are formed of the Borrowdale Volcanic series – ashes and lavas which break into large blocks of rock and weather into very rough textures. To the south, around Coniston and Windermere, a succession of Silurian grits, slates, flags and limestone can be traced. In the western half of the Lake District there are massive intrusions of granitic rocks, notably in Eskdale and Ennerdale, with less prominent intrusions around the Skiddaw Fells in the north and the Shap Fells in the east. The whole fringe of the Lake District is surrounded by Carboniferous limestone bands, as well as by coal measures, sandstones, shales and grits. Despite the varied layers of rock, the fundamental shape of the Lake District was determined in the Ice Age, when glaciers widened and deepened existing valleys and scoured out the deep troughs which now hold the lakes and tarns.

History

In the Bronze Age the western half of the Lake District was well settled and aerial photographs reveal a number of sites featuring cairns, monuments and hut circles. The Romans are known to have penetrated the Lake District from Penrith to Ravenglass, and a string of their forts can still be inspected, along with traces of their roads. Following the departure of the Romans, the Dark Ages really do seem to have been dark in Lakeland, and there are few references to the region until the 12th century, although Norse placenames were certainly imposed before that time. The Normans came late into Cumbria and close on their heels came the establishment of monastic estates. It was from those times that large scale grazing became established. Family farming with secure tenure dates from the 16th century and the farmers were known as "statesmen". Mining and quarrying became more and more important, but the only real large scale developments occurred on the fringes of Lakeland.

Natural History

Originally, the Lake District was clothed in dense forest with only the highest peaks protruding above the trees. Lake margins were tangled with vegetation or featured areas of marshy ground. Despite its wilderness appearance today, the Lakeland fells have been well and truly tamed. Centuries of sheep grazing have prevented the tree cover from re-establishing itself, led to a decrease in plant species and contributed to erosion. Wiry grasses and heathers cover places where forests once grew, and only in a few places do stunted sessile oaks cling to rocky faces to remind visitors of those times.

All the peat seen on the broader fells and moorlands is made up of decayed plant remains and sometimes the roots and bark of long dead trees can be distinguished. Tree cover is being re-established, unfortunately with alien conifers in many instances, while introduced rhododendrons run riot in other areas.

As sheep graze back the grass cover, invasive bracken colonises whole fellsides. While a few species of deer are found in the Lake District, their presence in forests is a nuisance and they are likely to be shot. Foxes and badgers take their chances, and there are many packs of foxhounds loosed on the fells to be followed by their masters. Red squirrels have one of their last strongholds in the Lake District, but creatures such as the pine marten are barely holding on. Bird life is profuse, and many passage migrants can be spotted as they cross the narrow parts of northern England.

Weather

Lakeland weather is at best unpredictable.

Whatever the national weather forecasts may claim, mountainous areas generate their own brand of weather. Summers can be hot, but are not necessarily always hot. Likewise, winters can be cold, but sometimes weeks can pass without any snow cover. In a harsh winter, the fells can be truly arctic and no-one should venture into them unprepared. This can mean dressing in warm protective clothing, carrying full bivouac kit, as well as ice axe and crampons. In high summer, clear skies can cause intense heat and a combined danger of sunstroke and sunburn. This time, cool protective clothing, a hat with good shade, plenty of suncream and plenty to drink are required.

Waterproofs, spare dry clothes, and an alertness to the dangers of cold and hyperthermia are required. In mist, the ability to navigate carefully and accurately with a map and compass is essential.

Felltop weather forecasts can be obtained which are specifically drafted to take account of Lake District conditions. Weather notices are often posted at information centres and some car parks, and it is also possible to ring a recorded weather announcement on (017687) 75757 or (0891) 500419.

Advice to Walkers

The best advice is to tackle routes which are within your capabilities, and to turn back if you feel that you are in danger of exceeding your capabilities. Accidents generally happen when people don't take care about where they are heading, or try to do something which is beyond their capabilities.

Accidents are best avoided altogether by knowing what can go wrong and taking steps to ensure it can't go wrong. Minor cuts and grazes will be sustained at some point, so a basic first aid kit should be carried. Adding further items to take care of more serious trouble is a good idea. You may not need them, but someone else might.

If the worst comes to the worst and there is a serious accident needing professional help, then there are courses of action to be followed. If you are walking alone, then you need to summon help from anyone who might be passing. This is generally done by blowing the International Mountain Distress Signal from a whistle. If you have companions, then some can stay with you while others go for help. Help is readily summoned from the nearest telephone, or from a mobile phone, by dialling 999 and asking for the Mountain Rescue. At this point let the experts take over and do exactly as you are told.

Access

Throughout England and Wales, access comes in many guises. Public rights of way include footpaths, bridleways and byways. There are also permitted paths and access areas, where there may be occasional restrictions on use. In the Lake District, there is a long tradition of virtual free access to the fells. This freedom comes with immense responsibilities and there must never be any abuse of it. All the land in the Lake District is owned by someone. Walkers have a right of passage across that land when they are following rights of way. Walkers are allowed on to permitted paths and access areas, subject to any restrictions that might be in force. The presence of walkers on most of the rugged fell tops and fellsides has long been accepted, but is not a right. There is no right to pitch a tent anywhere without permission, though in many secluded places on the high fells an overnight pitch will be tolerated provided that no damage or litter is caused. It is in the interests of all walkers to be extremely respectful of all the land they cross, and to be friendly and polite to those whose land and livelihood it is.

Maps

A map covering the whole of the Lake District on a single sheet is likely to be too simple or too cluttered with detail for it to be of any great use. Ordnance Survey produce useful maps at scales of 1:50,000 and 1:25,000. The 1:50,000 maps are known as Landranger Maps, and the Lake District is covered by sheets 89, 90, 96 and 97. The 1:25,000 maps are known as Outdoor Leisure Maps and the Lake District is covered by sheets 4, 5, 6 and 7. This does not offer complete coverage of the area, and some peripheral parts need to be supplemented by 1:25,000 scale Pathfinder Maps.

Another publisher of maps is Harvey Map Services, who produce detailed maps at scales of 1:40,000 and 1:25,000. The 1:40,000 maps are known as The Walker's Map, while the 1:25,000 maps are known as Superwalkers. Titles in both series include Northern, North-Western, Southern, Central and Eastern.

Distances and Height Gain

The walks in this guidebook range from 4 to 10¼ miles (6 to 17km). Average walkers will not have any difficulty completing any of them in a day, and many may be completed in a morning or an afternoon.

It is important not only to look at the distance, but also at the height gain. The height gain can be as little as 150ft/50m, or as great as 3,700ft/1,125m. A combination of the distance and the height gain can give some idea of the time needed to complete any particular walk, but the nature of the terrain is also important.

Individual approaches to walking cause even more variation – lengthy lunch breaks, frequent stops to admire the view, or lengthy discussions with companions. The time allowance is merely a guide and should be adjusted in the light of individual performance. It generally refers to the time needed to complete the walk without too much hurry, but without any allowance for stops along the way.

Getting There

In past centuries, few would have risked venturing to the Lake District, but in modern times road and rail transport make the journey easy and straight forward. Although the rail network has been reduced from its former glory, visitors can still reach Penrith, Kendal, Windermere, Grange-over-Sands, Ulverston, and all points along the West Cumbria Coast. There are National Express coach services into the Lake District, serving places such as Kendal, Windermere and Keswick. Travelling to the area by car is facilitated by good motorway and main road approaches, but there is a danger of grinding to a halt at Lakeland bottlenecks in peak periods.

Getting Around

Once inside the Lake District, most of the bus services are operated by Cumberland, which is part of the Stagecoach Group. There are also important Post Bus services to some remote parts, while the Ravenglass & Eskdale Railway provides a novel route through Eskdale. In some areas, Lake steamer services could be used to join or leave a particular walk. Full details of all public transport options within the Lake District can be obtained from a helpline number (01228) 606000.

Some of the larger car parks around the Lake District make heavy charges for parking, while many of the smaller car parks can quickly become crowded. Carelessly parked cars have resulted in traffic jams and consequent delays to public transport and emergency services. Visiting walkers should consider leaving their cars at home and using the public transport network.

Where to Stay

There is abundant accommodation in the Lake District, but the area is notorious for crowding at peak times and it can sometimes be very difficult to find lodgings. There are campsites, bunkhouses, youth hostels, B&Bs and hotels, not to mention self-catering cottages and caravans. Wise walkers will book their beds in advance and enquire about local facilities. If searching for accommodation at the last minute, the best plan is to go to one of the Tourist Information Centres and see if they can ring around and book a bed. They will often do this for a set fee or a percentage of the booking fee. It saves a protracted and frustrating session in a phone box. With more time to plan ahead, there are all sorts of handbooks and brochures listing accommodation which can be studied at leisure.

Tourist Information

There are two types of information centres in the Lake District. Tourist Information Centres are usually provided by local authorities, while National Park Centres are provided by the National Park Authority. Generally, it is the Tourist Information Centres which are best able to handle accommodation bookings and provide visitors with a comprehensive coverage of facilities, things to do and things to see. The National Park Centres are better able to supply details relating to the ideals of the National Park, conservation, wildlife, etc. Both types of centres will stock maps and guides, or may be the starting point for informative guided walks.

WHINLATTER

The Whinlatter Pass, which is crossed between Braithwaite and Lorton, separates two distinct ranges of fells. To the north of the pass are the Whinlatter Fells, which are fairly low, with forested flanks and open summits. To the south of the pass, the Coledale Fells rise higher and their forested flanks quickly give way to steep slopes of scree. Coledale is surrounded by fine fells, with Grisedale Pike assuming a lordly, conical form.

Keswick is the nearest large town, but the village of Braithwaite is closer to both of the walks in this section. There are frequent bus services passing through Braithwaite, with a less frequent summer service crossing the Whinlatter Pass. Looking at the fells from Keswick, the fine lines of the Coledale Fells more readily catch the eye than do the lumpy lines of the Whinlatter Fells. The eye is often misled and few fells offer such a dramatic view as lowly Barf in the Whinlatter Fells. Then again, few horseshoe walks are as perfectly formed as the Coledale Horseshoe.

Make the most of the Whinlatter Forest Visitor Centre, where it is possible to learn all about forestry in the Lake District, from its very beginning. The walk from the centre is unusual in that it follows numbered waymark posts which form a useful navigational aid. None of the other routes in this book offer an "ascent by numbers" description. The walk around the Coledale Horseshoe is one of the classic Lakeland fell walks, with an option to climb up on to Grasmoor from its "easy" side.

While there are no facilities on either of these walks, there are refreshments to be had at the starting points. The Whinlatter Forest Visitor Centre includes a restaurant, while the village of Braithwaite boasts a couple of fine inns. Keswick has of course a full range of facilities and can be visited immediately after completing either of the walks. Keswick also has an excellent Tourist Information Centre in the middle of town in the Moot Hall.

The woodcock

The Lake District is dotted with oddities and the enquiring walker can spot all sorts of things while crossing the fells. On these walks look out for the Bishop of Barf, strange sculptures lurking in Whinlatter Forest, as well as the waterfalls of Low Force, High Force and the Force Crag mines. In clear weather, let the eye range across lakes and airy ridges to the distant Pennines and southern Scotland.

Christine Isherwood

1 Whinlatter Forest

Travellers on the road between Keswick and Cockermouth are sometimes intrigued to spot a white stump of rock on the steep slopes of Barf. This is the Bishop of Barf, a resistant relic of rock which receives an annual whitewash from patrons of the Swan Hotel. An ascent of Barf can be made from Whinlatter Forest – the oldest Forestry Commission plantation. Tracks and paths are clearly depicted on the Forestry Commission's Whinlatter Pass Guide Map, and numbered posts have been planted at junctions to allow for easier route-finding.

Distance: 5 miles/8km	tracks and hill paths marked by numbered posts.
Height gain: 1,640ft/500m	
Walking time: 3 hours	**Start/Finish:** Visitor Centre car park.
Type of walk: Forest	GR208245.

Whinlatter is the oldest Forestry Commission plantation. The first tree planted by the commission was in London, but the first plantation was established in 1919 on the slopes of Grisedale Pike. It is known as Hospital Plantation, as there was once an isolation hospital beside the road.

Leave the Visitor Centre and pass a nearby white house. Look out for numbered junctions 15, 14 and 13 while following a broad track, turning left at number 13. Watch out for a path on the right which suddenly drops down from the track, following the course of Comb Beck downstream. The beck needs to be forded at one point, then when a broad track is reached, turn left. The track runs gently downhill, passing close to the village of Thornthwaite, leading down to a minor road at junction number 18.

Turn left to follow a narrow minor road towards a farm. It is possible to continue along this road to reach the Swan Hotel for food and drink. If a visit to the hotel isn't required, turn left before the road reaches a ford and cross a stile. Follow a path which leads uphill through Beckstones Plantation, looking out from the trees to spot the whitewashed figure of the Bishop of Barf on a steep slope of scree. At the foot of the steep slope, often hidden in the undergrowth, is a slender spike of white-washed rock known as the Clerk. A direct ascent of Barf by way of the Clerk and Bishop is not recommended as the steep slopes bear unstable scree and loose vegetation in places.

The forest path steepens as it crosses a short rocky bar, then a more mature part of Beckstones Plantation is entered where some tall trees were toppled by strong winds in the past. A track is joined at junction 21, where a short walk to the right leads to the edge of the forest. Cross a stile over the forest fence to reach open ground, and follow a narrow path across the course of Beckstones Gill. The path runs up slopes of grass and heather to reach the summit of Barf at 1,536ft/468m.

Although only a lowly fell, Barf features a wide-ranging view which stretches all the way into southern Scotland. The vast, rounded bulk of Skiddaw dominates the view to the east, while the full length of Bassenthwaite Lake is spread out immediately below. The wooded near shores of Bassenthwaite Lake contrast with the patchwork of fields stretching away from the far shore. There is a great feeling of depth to this view, so that more distant features are scarcely noticed.

A hummocky and occasionally boggy crest leads towards the neighbouring fell of Lord's Seat. There is a path leading along the crest, allowing walkers to reach the 1,811ft/552m summit in a matter of a few minutes. A pair of old iron fenceposts protrude from the top of Lord's Seat, which is the highest of the Whinlatter Fells. Views are fairly extensive, stretching along the Scafell and Helvellyn ranges, still featuring southern Scotland, but not nearly as arresting or spacious as the view from nearby Barf.

Leave the summit of Lord's Seat by walking down to a fence and cross over a stile. A stony path has been floated across an area of bog on a raft of logs, where only a few trees have ever been planted. At junction number 5, turn right and follow a narrow path which later widens as it descends into the forest. Keep to the broadest track throughout the descent until junction 3 is reached at Tarbarrel Moss. Turn left at this junction and descend more steeply along a broad track to an information board at junction 2. A feature is made of the view towards the pyramidal peak of Grisedale Pike. Hospital Plantation, dating from 1919, can be studied.

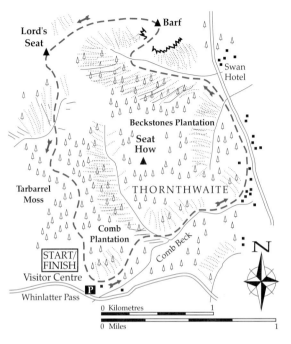

Walk straight down a narrow track, turning left along a path which leads back towards the Visitor Centre. There are a couple of strange wooden sculptures lurking in the forest and these are worth searching for as the walk draws to a close. The network of paths and tracks allows for all sorts of variations and extensions to the walk. Refreshments are available at the end of the walk at the restaurant.

2 Coledale Horseshoe

This is one of the classic Lakeland horseshoe walks, offering a high-level circuit around the glaciated valley of Coledale, following delightful ridge paths over a succession of summits. High points include Grisedale Pike, Hopegill Head, Crag Hill, Sail and Causey Pike, although there is scope to include bulky Grasmoor in the round, too. In case of bad weather or fatigue, there are early descents available, and any descent made from the head of Coledale includes views of splendid waterfalls pouring over the precipitous Force Crag.

Distance:
9 miles/15.5km
Height gain:
3,700ft/1,125m
Walking time: 6 hours
Type of walk:
Fellwalking, following

fairly clear, dry, high-level paths.
Start/Finish: *On the Whinlatter road, above Braithwaite village. GR227237.*

Braithwaite is just off the busy road between Keswick and Cockermouth, and its streets are constricted. If arriving by bus, then walk up the Whinlatter road a short way. If arriving by car, then drive up the road and use a tiny car park in a small quarry on the left-hand side of the road.

A small sign at the car park indicates the way to Grisedale Pike, and steps lead up through the bracken which covers the fellside. There are a few trees on the slope, then the path bends left and reaches a level area where a stile is crossed. Continue treading along the path which runs parallel to a forest fence to climb up the next part of the ridge towards the hump of Kinn.

The path drifts away from the forest fence and the ground levels out for a while. The next steep slope features a change of vegetation from bracken to heather, and as more height is gained on the ridge of Sleet How the underlying rock begins to protrude more noticeably from the ground. The steep climb bears an obvious path which leads straight to the stony summit of Grisedale Pike at 2,539ft/791m.

Leave Grisedale Pike by following the ridge path running south-west. This is accompanied by the scanty remains of a fence. A minor summit is crossed by a tumbled wall before a gap is crossed above Hobcarton Crag. In mist, take care not to be drawn along a path which descends to Coledale Hause, but keep to the right, where a short ascent leads to the summit of Hopegill Head at 2,525ft/770m.

While it is tempting to follow the ridge onwards towards Whiteside, this leads well off the course of the Coledale Horseshoe. Follow a path roughly southwards across the hump of Sand Hill, and continue down to the low-slung gap of Coledale Hause around 1,970ft/600m. This gap is an obvious escape route; a path and track run along the length of Coledale to return to Braithwaite if any walkers need to retire early.

To continue the horseshoe walk, climb uphill following a path between Crag Hill, to the left, and Grasmoor, to the right. The path accompanies the headwaters of Gasgale Gill and levels out on the broad gap of Wandope Moss. Turn left at this point and a path can be followed quite easily on to the summit of Crag Hill, which reaches 2,749ft/840m. This is the highest point reached on the circuit, although it is slightly lower than neighbouring Grasmoor. The view takes in most of the prominent Lakeland Fells, although these are best appreciated by wandering around the rim of the broad, stony summit.

Take a path running roughly eastwards to descend a short, steep ridge leading to a narrow gap. A slight ascent leads across Sail, whose summit reaches 2,530ft/771m. The path runs downhill to Sail Pass, where there is an option of an early descent along a path to the left. Staying high, however, the ridge path climbs slightly to pass the 2,205ft/672m summit of Scar Crags on the way to Causey Pike. Causey Pike is the final 'nail' in the horseshoe, and its crest features camel's humps rising to a high point of 2,090ft/637m. There is great depth to the view as the slopes seem to plummet in all directions, while further afield many notable Lakeland Fells can be identified.

Follow the ridge path steeply downhill to Sleet Hause, then aim to keep high as far as Rowling End before continuing steeply downhill to the road. This makes the view last for as long as possible. All that remains is to turn left and follow the road back to Braithwaite. The return can be

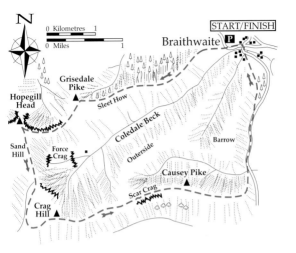

varied slightly by following a bridleway up a wooded brow above the road, passing through a little gap to reach Braithwaite Lodge, then following the access road down to Braithwaite village. Keep left in the village to follow the Whinlatter road back to the small car park where the walk started.

Anyone descending early via the path from Sail Pass to Barrow Door can choose either to continue down to High Coledale and Braithwaite, or climb over the fell of Barrow and descend to Braithwaite by way of Braithwaite Lodge. There are places to eat and drink in Braithwaite, but in any case Keswick is nearby and offers a full range of facilities.

KESWICK

Keswick is the Lake District's major town, nestling in a verdant vale with fine fells on all sides. Its main street is dominated by the Moot Hall, which houses the Tourist Information Centre, offering a wealth of knowledge about the surrounding area. Outdoor gear shops and craft shops abound, along with a good supply of pubs, restaurants and cafes. There is a full range of accommodation from camp sites to large hotels.

This book covers half of the Lake District and as the dividing line runs through Keswick, only walks to the south of the town are described. There are three walks in this section, spread across the Newlands Valley and Derwent Water, regarded by many walkers as one of the most charming areas of the Lake District.

Newlands is a quiet little valley dotted with farmsteads and threaded by a few minor roads. There is no public transport, so you must either use a car to approach the dale, or walk in from Keswick. One walk takes in the towering fells of Robinson and Hindscarth, which dominate Newlands, another walk traverses the fine ridge from High Spy to Cat Bells, offering views across both Newlands and Derwent Water. The third walk is a popular excursion from Keswick, taking in the shores of Derwent Water and the rugged prow of Walla Crag. All the walks feature magnificent views of lofty Skiddaw, which is covered in the companion volume to this book.

This is a landscape of literary note. William Wordsworth, John Ruskin, Hugh Walpole and Beatrix Potter are among scores of poets and writers who have penned lines about the area; each in remarkably different styles. Strange that there should be no writers' museum in Keswick, for there are other museums dealing with art, railways, cars and even pencils!

Keswick is the terminus for a number of bus services. Walkers who arrive without a car will not be inconvenienced if they obtain timetable details. There are all year round services towards Penrith, Cockermouth, Ambleside and Borrowdale, with summer services running across Whinlatter Pass to reach Buttermere. By using bus services and taking careful note of their running times, walks need not always be circular, but can be extended across whole ranges of fells to link with an appropriate service back to Keswick.

Christine Isherwood

Skiddaw from Cat Bells

3 Littledale

The verdant Newlands Valley splits into a number of wilder upper dales, one of which is Littledale. Ridges on either side of Littledale run up to the summits of Robinson and Hindscarth – fells which are more commonly climbed from Buttermere. The circuit around Littledale can be accomplished from the hamlet of Little Town. "Once upon a time," wrote Beatrix Potter, "there was a little girl called Lucie, who lived at a farm called Little Town." This is indeed the place, and Lucie's father was the vicar at nearby Newlands Church.

Distance:	moderate fellwalk,
7¼ miles/12km	featuring a few awkward
Height gain:	rock steps on the ascent.
2,460ft/750m	**Start/Finish:** Between
Walking time: 5 hours	Newlands Church and
Type of walk: A	Little Town. GR233194.

Beatrix Potter's Mrs Tiggy-Winkle may not be spotted on this walk, but views from the higher summits embrace most of the Lakeland Fells. William Wordsworth penned some charming lines about Newlands Church, and Hugh Walpole made use of the area in his "Herries" novels. With all this literary background some sort of theme park might be expected, but this is the Lake District at its most charming, featuring only farmsteads and fells.

Cars can be parked between Little Town and

Newlands Church, and the walk begins by following the narrow road uphill from the old whitewashed church to the farm of High Snab.

Walk straight past the farm and continue along a walled track to reach the open dale head beyond. Turn right to follow a path which climbs steeply up slopes of bracken to reach the top of High Snab Bank. Turn left to climb more gently along the crest of the ridge for a while.

The great bulk of Robinson rises ahead, and by following this particular ridge there is a series of rugged rock steps to cross which needs care. This is not rock climbing, but hands as well as feet will need to be used from time to time. Watch for the most obvious signs of passage while climbing. The path proceeds further uphill close to the edge of Robinson Crags, where care again needs to be exercised. A couple of prominent cairns seem to suggest that the summit is close at hand, but there is more climbing beyond them. As the gradient begins to ease the broad, stony, domed summit of Robinson is finally reached. The cairn on top stands at 2,417ft/737m, and the name of the fell supposedly relates to a Richard Robinson who bought it in the 16th century.

The view after all the effort is indeed wide-ranging, stretching from the North Pennines to southern Scotland, as well as taking in many fine Lakeland Fells.

Walk a short way southwards from the summit until a fence is reached. Turn left to follow it further downhill and across a broad gap above Littledale

Edge. The path climbs gently uphill from the gap, and it is important to remember to bear left to reach the summit of Hindscarth, and not to be drawn off course towards the summit of Dale Head in the distance. (It is possible to include a visit to Dale Head and return to Hindscarth afterwards, at a cost of an extra 2 miles/3km.)

The highest part of Hindscarth bears a cairn at 2,385ft/727m. As this point is gained, the view northwards over the Newlands Valley towards the Vale of Keswick and Skiddaw is good, and the walk continues in that general direction. On reaching another prominent cairn, reputed to be a burial cairn, the view suddenly becomes exceptional, featuring a sense of depth and interest which is largely lacking from the summit of the fell.

The path leading downhill follows a ridge which is steep and stony in places, but it later levels out for a while. Do not be tempted to short-cut either to Scope Beck or Newlands Beck as there are some dangerous crags on the flanks of the fell. May Crag and High Crags are to be avoided altogether. The ridge walk continues at a fairly gentle gradient as far as Scope End, from which rocky slopes fall away in all directions. A path leads safely down the final steep and rocky slope towards the farm of Low Snab.

Spoil heaps close to Low Snab indicate the site of Goldscope Mine, which once produced abundant copper and lead ore, as well as a little silver. It is rumoured that gold was also found, and hence the name, but apparently it was worked by German miners who referred to it as 'Gottesgab' – or God's gift. Untapped resources remain, but the cost of pumping water from the main shaft cut the profit margins and the site has long been abandoned.

Teas and snacks may be obtained at Low Snab Farm, otherwise follow the access road back towards Newlands Church and turn right for Little Town.

4 High Spy and Cat Bells

When seen from the shores of Derwent Water near Keswick, Cat Bells appears as a mini-Matterhorn as its pyramidal peak soars skywards from the lake. Many walkers aspire to reach its summit and although the ascent is unremittingly steep, it is also within the capability of most people. Some walkers continue onwards following an obvious ridge path to Maiden Moor and High Spy. To enjoy the finest views the walk is best accomplished in the other direction, and Little Town in the Newlands Valley offers the quietest approaches.

Distance:	*tracks and paths along a*
8 miles/13km	*fairly well defined ridge*
Height gain:	*with some steep slopes.*
2,050ft/625m	***Start/Finish:*** *Car park*
Walking time: *5 hours*	*south of Little*
Type of walk: *Clear*	*Town.GR234195.*

This walk starts at Little Town and saves the summit of Cat Bells until the end. First, Newlands Beck is followed to its head in a wild dale before a steady ascent leads on to High Spy. From there a fine ridge walk is suspended between the Newlands Valley and Derwent Water, offering splendid views before the ascent of Cat Bells.

Start at the small car park just outside Little Town

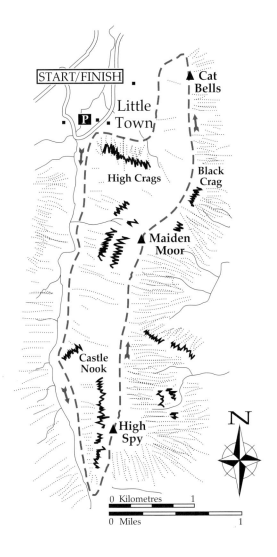

START/FINISH

Cat
Bells

P

Little
Town

High Crags

Black
Crag

Maiden
Moor

Castle
Nook

High
Spy

N

0 Kilometres   1

0 Miles   1

33

on the way to Newlands church. This is a lovely, tranquil, pastoral landscape long settled by "statesmen" farmers. It is featured in the writings of many literary figures.

Just south of Little Town, a track branches left from the minor road, and a National Trust sign reads simply "Newlands". Follow this broad and obvious track all the way to the head of the Newlands valley, passing a solitary building used by the Carlisle Mountaineering Club. After passing the club hut, the track begins to climb more steeply.

Once the hut has been lost from the view, branch left, climbing more steeply along another path. There is a small cairn perched on a rock marking this junction. The path leads across a bouldery fellside, aiming for a gap between the rugged fells of Dale Head and High Spy. As you emerge on to this gap, swing to the left to follow a path towards High Spy. The summit cairn is soon reached and stands at 2,143ft/653m.

High Spy with my little eye ... a fine panorama of fells. The Scafell, Skiddaw and Helvellyn groups are featured, along with the fells around Buttermere. The summit area is fairly flat, though it drops precipitously into the Newlands valley. Walk towards the edge of the crags for a better view into the wilder, upper reaches of Newlands.

There is a fine path blazed along the crest of High Spy, where small lumps of rock protrude all along the ridge. The wiry grass cover gives way to heather on Narrow Moor – an appropriate name for the narrow crest between High Spy and

Maiden Moor, or between Newlands and Borrowdale, depending on the point of view of the walker. The ground broadens out again as Maiden Moor is crossed. The path forks, and it is necessary to keep left to reach the summit at 1,887ft/576m. The path to the right misses the summit, but still keeps on course towards Cat Bells.

Whichever path is followed across Maiden Moor, a moderately steep descent along a blunt ridge leads to the gap of Hause Gate. Devotees of Hugh Walpole's *Herries* novels will find Hause Gate a good point from which to note many places associated with the stories. Exit leftwards to Little Town for an early descent.

Continuing to Cat Bells involves one final ascent, which is neither too long nor too steep. The 1,481ft/451m summit is devoid of vegetation, having been trodden down to bare rock.

The view across the Vale of Keswick, Derwent Water and Borrowdale is charming, and fine fells rise from the low ground. Skiddaw and Blencathra catch the eye, the length of the Helvellyn range is in view, while the peaks and ridges around the Coledale Horseshoe feature well.

Follow the path northwards to descend from the summit. The first section is steep and badly eroded, and so needs care. When the path runs along a more level ridge, turn left and follow another path which zigzags down into the Newlands valley. This path reaches a wall on the bracken clad slopes of the lower fellside, where a left turn leads back towards Little Town.

5 Walla Crag

There are many who would not consider themselves fellwalkers, and yet think nothing of climbing Walla Crag above Derwent Water near Keswick. The precipitous face and rugged, wooded slopes falling towards the lake give the crag an air of inaccessibility, but this is an illusion. There is an easy ascent from Keswick, and a moderate climb from the famous Ashness Bridge. A stretch of Derwent Water's shore can be combined with this short fellwalk, so that the scenery continually changes and entrances the walker.

Distance: 7 miles/11km	lakeshore stroll and easy fellwalk, mostly on good clear paths.
Height gain: 985ft/300m	**Start/Finish:** The Moot Hall, Keswick.
Walking time: 4 hours	GR266234.
Type of walk: A	

Keswick is a bustling Lakeland town with everything a walker needs. The Moot Hall stands in the centre of town, offering tourist information and an occasional series of evening slide shows about the Lake District.

Start the walk by following Lake Road which leads towards the lake. An underpass is used on the way to a car park, which some motorists may prefer to use in preference to the town centre car parks.

Lake Road is traffic free as it runs towards the

shores of Derwent Water. A broad track and path lead onwards to Friar's Crag, which is a wooded rocky promontory projecting into the lake. A fine view takes in Cat Bells, Walla Crag and the Jaws of Borrowdale.

John Ruskin recalled: "The first thing which I remember as an event in my life was being taken by my nurse to the brow of Friar's Crag on Derwent Water." A monument to Ruskin has been planted in the mixed woodland which adorns the point.

Go completely around Friar's Crag, then along a stretch of lakeshore path. This leads alongside fields, passing mature trees, before moving away from the lake and running through a woodland. A track is suddenly reached, where a right turn is made before the lakeshore path is regained. There are views towards St. Herbert's Island, where St. Herbert lived as a hermit and was occasionally visited by St. Cuthbert of Lindisfarne.

The path remains faithful to the shore of Derwent Water, even though the road is sometimes alongside. Step up on to the road at Barrow Bay, and take the narrow road on the left which climbs uphill towards Watendlath. This road runs up to Ashness Bridge, much beloved of photographers, artists and postcard manu-facturers. Well it might be, for it is indeed a lovely stone span with a delightful scenic backdrop of Derwent Water and lofty Skiddaw. Nearby is a small memorial to Bob Graham, a fellrunner who in June 1932 ran 72 miles over 42 Lakeland fells in less than 24 hours. The record stood unbroken for 28 years.

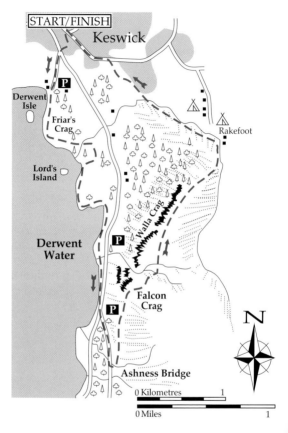

On the lower side of Ashness Bridge, follow a path which runs upstream, before turning left along another path. A ladder stile is crossed before the path continues climbing towards Walla Crag. After the initial steep and rugged slopes, there is a gentler stroll around the headwaters of Cat Gill before Walla Crag is reached.

Cross over a wall on the left to make the most of the splendid view from the summit, which stands at 1,234ft/376m. Rocky and wooded slopes fall towards Derwent Water, beyond which rise Cat Bells and Maiden Moor. The bulky form of Skiddaw dominates the town of Keswick, and other fine fells are seen across the Newlands Valley. Part of the Helvellyn and Scafell ranges are also in view, but it is the sense of depth and the nearby prospects which are most notable from Walla Crag.

Cross back over the wall and continue walking alongside the wall, following it downhill towards Brockle Beck. Cross a footbridge to reach the farm at Rakefoot and turn left to follow the access road for a short while. A path leads down from the left side of the road to cross Brockle Beck again using another footbridge. A woodland path can be followed beside the beck – sometimes running high above it on a steep banking. When a farmyard is reached, the beck is crossed by road, and the road can be followed all the way back into Keswick. The road leads straight back to the Moot Hall in the centre of town.

BUTTERMERE

Buttermere is a splendid dale with instant access to several superb ranges of fells, or to three lovely lakeshore strolls. There is only a summer bus service through the dale, running from Keswick, so outside that time approaches need to be either by car or on foot. Facilities are rather limited and at peak times it is a good idea to book accommodation well in advance. Along the length of the dale there are only a few places offering food or drink.

Four walks are offered in this section, encompassing the fells ranged all around the dale and including a couple of easier walks. The huge form of Grasmoor, which dominates the mid-part of the dale, can be climbed with relative ease via Gasgale and Coledale Hause. The return towards Buttermere takes in an airy ridge walk over Whiteless Pike.

The long-tailed tit

Christine Isherwood

The trek along the High Stile range is one of the classic Lakeland fell walks and it concludes with a walk along the lovely shore of Buttermere. Haystacks and Fleetwith Pike rise from the head of the dale and a rugged walk takes in both summits.

The final walk is a gentle stroll around the shores

of Buttermere, which must be one of the easiest walks in the Lake District.

Walkers can finish their explorations in the tiny village of Buttermere, where there are two pubs and a cafe offering food and drink. There is a chance to check out the story of the "Maid of Buttermere", or simply relax and review the day's walk. The Ramblers' Association has long had a holiday base at Hassness and there are Youth Hostels at Buttermere and on top of the Honister Pass. Beyond these few facilities there are only a handful of farmsteads.

Some walkers may wish to pay silent tribute to the late Alfred Wainwright as they cross the rugged crest of Haystacks. The old fellwalker and celebrated guidebook writer asked for no memorial to be raised in his memory, but he did ask for his ashes to be scattered on the fell. "And if you, dear reader," he wrote, "should get a bit of grit in your boot as you are crossing Haystacks in the years to come, please treat it with respect. It might be me."

6 Grasmoor

The huge, bulky fell of Grasmoor raises its rugged ramparts above Crummock Water and frowns on fellwalkers who dare to contemplate an ascent. While it is true that a direct ascent of the steep slopes would bring some walkers quickly to their knees, there is a relatively gentle way to the summit from the other side. The canyon-like gash of Gasgale is the key to a moderate ascent, while a ridge route can later be taken down via Whiteless Pike.

Distance:	moderate fellwalk using
9 miles/14.5km	good paths, but with care
Height gain:	needed in mist.
2,525ft/770m	**Start/Finish:**
Walking time: 5 hours	Lanthwaite Green.
Type of walk: A	GR159209.

Lanthwaite Green is an open area of common beside the road running from Lorton to Buttermere. Parking is available beside the road at the very foot of Grasmoor. When driving through, keep an eye open for sheep on the road. A farmer was moved to erect a sign reading "Tek care – lambs on t'road", which was promptly photographed and issued in postcard form throughout the Lake District. This was followed by another sign reading "Leuk oot – yows aboot!"

Follow a path across the low, green common towards Gasgale, and cross a footbridge spanning

Gasgale Gill. Turn right to start walking upstream. There is a path trodden alongside the gill, although strictly speaking the right of way runs at a slightly higher elevation. The lower path, however, is perhaps rather more interesting and scenic. Shortly after leaving the footbridge, there are a couple of rocksteps to be negotiated, where hands need to be used for short stretches. If this is likely to prove a problem, then use the higher path when starting the walk.

There are many fine little waterfalls along the length of Gasgale Gill, and a fine view back through the mouth of Gasgale towards Mellbreak. Later, after turning around a couple of bends in the rugged dale, there is a feeling of being completely enclosed by the steep, scarred slopes. Keep walking upstream along a path which is free of any difficulties, to reach the broad and grassy gap of Coledale Hause around 1,970ft/600m.

There are all sorts of paths crossing Coledale Hause, but simply bear to the right and continue tracing Gasgale Gill upstream. There are places where the stream has occasionally burst its banks and followed the course of the path instead, strewing it with gravel. The path climbs from Coledale Hause, turning to the right, to reach a higher, grassy gap at Wandope Moss, between Crag Hill and Grasmoor. At this point a right turn can be taken towards Grasmoor, although anyone beginning to feel tired can omit the walk to the summit of the fell.

A fairly gentle climb up the grassy rump of

Grasmoor leads onto a broad summit area, where a cairn stands at 2,791ft/852m. Views are remarkably extensive, including sizeable stretches of southern Scotland and a peep towards the Pennines. It is worth walking around the edge of the broad summit area to make the most of nearby views.

A direct descent to Lanthwaite Green could be contemplated, but it is steep enough to cause knees to complain. For a gentler descent, start by retracing steps to the gap of Wandope Moss. Turn right at an intersection of paths and follow the crest of Whiteless Edge towards the knobbly little summit of Whiteless Pike. From this 2,159ft/660m viewpoint, the ground falls away steeply and views across Buttermere to the Scafells prove remarkable.

There is only one clear path descending from Whiteless Pike towards Buttermere, although this is eroded and braided in places. Take the descent steadily at first, until the slope eases above Whiteless Breast. There is another short descent towards Low Bank, where a variety of paths head off in all directions through the bracken.

Turn right and follow a path down into Rannerdale – the little dale in between Rannerdale Knotts and Whiteless Pike. The path follows Squat Beck downstream, which needs to be crossed later. Aim to follow the fellside path gradually downhill, to reach the roadside at Cinderdale Common.

Either turn right to follow the road back to Lanthwaite Green, or walk on the strip of common

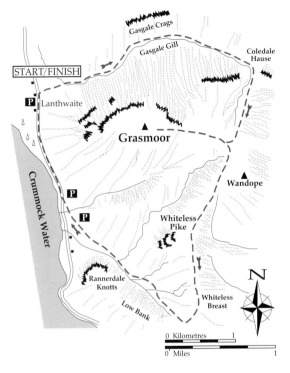

beside the road, away from the traffic, although there are some boggy areas to cross on the fellside.

In the summer months there is an occasional minibus service along the road, linking Buttermere with Keswick. The route can easily be restructured to make Buttermere the start and finish, although it would involve an extra short climb to Low Bank at the beginning.

7 High Stile

When viewed from Buttermere the High Stile range rises like a wall of rock towards the sky, wooded at the foot and streaming with becks pouring from a series of high corries. Direct ascents look steep, rough and tough – and indeed they are. There is a route to Red Pike which climbs uphill via Scale Force, and this has rather more acceptable gradients. The ridge can be walked from Red Pike to High Stile and High Crag, with knobbly Hay Stacks as an optional extra.

Distance: 9 miles/14.5km	rugged fellwalk with some steep and eroded paths needing care.
Height gain: 3,100ft/945m	**Start/Finish:**
Walking time: 6 hours	Buttermere village.
Type of walk: A high,	GR175169.

From Buttermere, the sight of the path leading towards Red Pike is enough to put a crick in the neck, and the summit isn't even visible from the village! A direct ascent up the face of the fell has already been ruled out, so do not be dismayed at the appearance of the fell. Leave Buttermere by keeping to the left of the Fish Hotel, following a clear and obvious track. Later, turn right along another track to reach the lovely stone arch of Scale Bridge.

urn right after crossing the bridge and follow a ough and stony path along the foot of a wooded lope. This path gradually climbs uphill, crossing a lope featuring stunted thorns and boulders. Views pen up across Crummock Water, taking in Grasmoor, Robinson and other fells. Keep climbing, ven though the path becomes vague in places, to each the deep, dark, rocky gash containing Scale orce.

t is difficult to view Scale Force properly, and the ock bar beside the lower fall needs to be climbed o allow a closer approach. Some people might feel hat this was not worth the risk of a fall and injury, vhile others may simply shin up and move a bit urther into the ravine.

here is a steep and rugged path climbing uphill longside the ravine, and as height is gained the radient eases. The path later pulls away from cale Beck and climbs up a broad and heathery lope to reach the edge of Ling Comb. Continue phill, enjoying the views from the rocky edge on he final approach to the summit. The ground ecomes peppered with stones before the ,479ft/755m summit cairn on Red Pike is reached.

he panorama from the top of Red Pike is extensive, but 1ost walkers look along the lengths of Buttermere and Crummock Water, and at the fells around Buttermere nd Ennerdale. The ground falls away sharply towards uttermere, giving a great sense of depth to the view, nd that apparent all along the ridge across High Stile nd High Crag.

There should be no problem identifying the line of the ridge walk to High Stile. The way is well trodden and additionally marked by the remains of a former fence. Views down into the steep-sided corrie of Bleaberry Cove include the lovely little Bleaberry Tarn. Locating the highest part of High Stile takes a bit of elementary surveying, as there are a number of cairns scattered across its broad and knobbly top. The highest stands at 2,644ft/806m.

The view opens up all the time, but to be enjoyed at its best it is necessary to scout around the rugged edges of High Stile's summit. There is a particularly good point overlooking Buttermere where the ground falls precipitously and a bird's-eye view along the dale is obtained. This is the sort of viewpoint which is good to help plan future walks in the fells, as everything from the top to the bottom of many fells is well displayed.

In mist it is necessary to take care when leaving High Stile's broad and rocky top – if only to avoid an unexpected return to Red Pike! A fairly narrow and rugged ridge leads towards the hump of High Crag, and the remains of the former fence continue to help as the path is followed onwards. The ascent to the summit of High Crag is hardly noticeable and the topmost cairn stands at 2,443ft/744m.

The path running down from High Crag has been completely reconstructed. Follow it faithfully downhill without short-cutting any of the new zig zags.

When the ground levels out at the foot of the steep

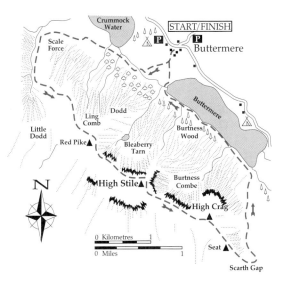

slope, there is the minor hump of Seat to cross, before another steep and rugged descent to Scarth Gap. Once this gap is reached, the route can either be cut short or extended across the crinkly summit of Hay Stacks.

Hay Stacks is covered in another route description which embraces neighbouring Fleetwith Pike, and both summits could be tagged on to the end of this walk along the High Stile range.

To return directly to Buttermere, however, is simply a matter of turning left on reaching Scarth Gap. A rough, but obvious path drifts gradually downhill across the steep fellside. There are two walls cutting across the path, before a final set of

49

zigzags take the path down to the floor of the dale. Don't walk across fields to the farm of Gatesgarth, but turn left to walk along a clear path along the foot of the High Stile range.

The path heads across the lower fellside to reach Burtness Wood, and it is possible to follow the shore of Buttermere closely on the way through the wood. Almost immediately on reaching the foot of the lake, turn right and cross a footbridge and follow the broad and obvious track through the pastures to return to Buttermere village.

In the summer time there is an occasional minibus service linking with places such as Whinlatter, Borrowdale and Keswick. There should be no rush to leave this charming little settlement, however, and given a clear evening it is possible to sit and review the day's walk across the high fells.

8 Hay Stacks

Tucked away at the head of Buttermere is a rugged little fell flanked on all sides by crags, with a host of summits liberally sprinkled with pools and small tarns. This is Hay Stacks, which a study of the map would lead many walkers to believe was simply a low point on an otherwise high level ridge. But Hay Stacks provides plenty of entertainment in its own right, and on this walk it is linked with neighbouring Fleetwith Pike above Honister Pass.

Distance: 5 miles/8km
Height gain: 2,460ft/750m
Walking time: 3 hours
Type of walk: A rugged *fellwalk with steep and rocky paths, needing care in mist.*
Start/Finish: *Gatesgarth Farm. GR195150.*

Fleetwith Pike and Hay Stacks have nothing in common with each other, apart from facing each other across the rugged dale head above Buttermere. Hay Stacks would often need to be pointed out to a walker new to the area, while Fleetwith Pike dominates the area easily by reason of its shape, bulk and situation.

Starting from the roadside car park at Gatesgarth near the head of Buttermere, Fleetwith Pike positively towers overhead and promises an unremitting slog to any walker who wants to make a direct ascent. The following route does not countenance such an ascent, though it would be wise to take note of the steep ridge in passing as it is used on the descent!

Walk past Gatesgarth Farm and across the lower pastures to cross Warnscale Beck at the foot of the High Stile range. Climb straight uphill above a wall, then later turn left to pass another wall. The course of a tumbledown wall is followed part way across the fellside, but later the path climbs higher to pass another wall before reaching more rugged slopes. The gradient is reasonably pitched, considering the steepness of the fellside.

Pause for a while when the path reaches the notch of Scarth Gap, in between High Crag and Hay Stacks. Turn left to pick a way up the steep and craggy slopes which flank Hay Stacks. Hands will need to be used on occasions as there are rocksteps to be climbed, but there is nothing too serious to be tackled. If in doubt stick to the course which shows the greatest evidence of use, which usually proves easier than trying to outflank any difficulties.

When the path begins to run at a gentler gradient, the top of Hay Stacks can be enjoyed – especially in clear weather. There is a clear path which works its way across the top of Hay Stacks, but by wandering off this line there are all sorts of interesting corners awaiting discovery. The true summit rises to 1,960ft/598m. Although views stretch away to the Scafell, Skiddaw and Helvellyn ranges, it is the nearby fells which feature the best seen soaring from their dale heads to their summits.

In clear weather there should be no problem forging a way along the rocky, heathery crest of Hay Stacks, but in mist the terrain can be confusing. Look for the tarn which is now known as the Innominate Tarn, and be sure to follow the clear path down towards nearby Blackbeck Tarn. Cross over the outflowing stream and continue across a rough and bleak moorland.

The path leads across the boggy Dubs Bottom, where the waters of Warnscale Beck are crossed. A slight climb leads up to Dubs Quarry, which is worth a few moments of careful exploration. From the quarry, simply take any line straight uphill on a rugged slope, aiming roughly northwards towards the crest of Fleetwith Pike. When a path is reached on the crest, turn left to follow it to the summit.

Although Fleetwith Pike looks like a pyramidal peak from some points, it is anything but at such close quarters. The summit cairn is at 2,126ft/640m, and when standing beside it there is a view along the length of Buttermere and Crummock Water, with the Grasmoor and High Stile ranges on either side. Great Gable and Pillar feature strongly, either side of Haystacks. Plenty of other fells are seen more distantly. Towards the edge of the fell, there is a dizzying drop towards Honister Pass.

The descent is straight down towards Buttermere. There is a path along the steep and rugged ridge, which is perfectly easy and safe if taken steadily. Predominantly rocky ground gives way to heather, which in turn gives way to grass and bracken – and all the time the lake draws nearer.

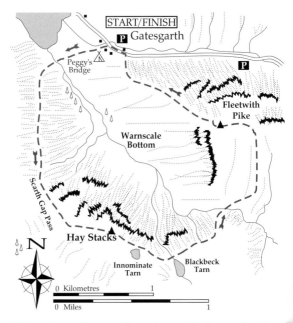

When Low Raven Crag is reached on the final stages of the descent, swing to the right to complete the walk down to the road. Look out for a white cross on the crag, which was planted in memory of Fanny Mercer, a girl who was killed on a family outing in 1887. The accident was curious because in those days it was advisable to carry a long alpenstock, and it was with this stick that the girl inadvertently pole vaulted over the cliff to her death.

With this sobering story, the walk is brought to a close back at the car park beside the road near Gatesgarth Farm.

9 Around Buttermere

The circuit of Buttermere is one of the classic short scenic walks in the Lake District. It seems to have everything - clear paths, easy gradients, spectacular fell scenery, beautiful lake scenery, woodlands, waterfalls, farms and fields. Most of the route is away from roads, but it proves popular with many walkers, so expect it to be quite busy in the summer. A tunnel has been cut through rock near Hassness, offering an unusual aspect to this walk.

Distance: 4 miles/6km
Height gain: 150ft/50m
Walking time: 2 hours
Type of walk: A pleasant and easy lakeshore stroll on good paths and tracks.
Start/Finish: Buttermere village. GR175169.

The term "The Beauty of Buttermere" is still heard these days, and it all began where this walk begins, at the Fish Hotel in Buttermere village. Mary Robinson lived at the hotel and it was she who was referred to as "The Beauty of Buttermere". Unfortunately, her beauty was her undoing, as in 1802 she attracted the attention of a man claiming to be The Honourable Colonel Alexander Augustus Hope. The man was an imposter, swindler and bigamist. He was exposed and hanged, leaving Mary with a child. She later married a farmer and is buried beyond the northern fells at Caldbeck.

Walk away from the car park beside the Fish Hotel, as if heading back into the village. Turn right when coming in sight of the little church, to follow the access track through Wilkinsyke Farm. An obvious and well surfaced path continues through fields to reach the shore of Buttermere, and a series of gates are used to pass through a number of fences.

As the wooded grounds around Hassness are approached, the path runs into a tunnel carved through rock. Apparently, it was created on the orders of George Benson, formerly of Hassness, so that he could walk all the way around Buttermere as close to the shore as possible.

Shortly after emerging from the tunnel, a road is joined which leads straight on past the head of the lake. Note the attractive line of pines planted along the head of Buttermere, which reflect beautifully when the lake surface is calm. Note also how Fleetwith Pike dominates the dale head and soars to dizzying heights. Turn right along the farm track leading across level meadows at Gatesgarth. Cross over a bridge spanning Warnscale Beck, then turn right to regain the shore of Buttermere.

The path runs along the foot of a rugged fellside, with the High Stile range towering above. The path enters Burtness Wood and there are two choices. One is to stay quite close to the lakeshore, while the other is to follow a path at a slightly higher elevation and follow the shore more closely later.

Either way, the lakeshore path reaches the foot of the lake, where a right turn leads across a bridge spanning the outflowing river. Most walkers simply follow a broad and obvious track back

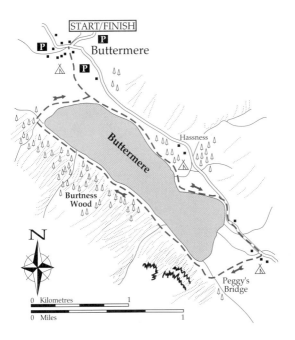

towards the village of Buttermere, and this is perfectly acceptable. However, a new stretch of lakeshore access was provided in recent years and some walkers may wish to make use of it to complete their circuit.

Simply stay faithful to the shore of the lake, following a barely trodden path around the foot of the lake, until a much clearer path is reached. This clear path was followed at the start of the walk, and by turning left it can be used to return to Buttermere village by way of Wilkinsyke Farm.

BORROWDALE

Running south from Keswick towards some of the highest fells in the Lake District is Borrowdale. The variety of scenery and walking throughout the dale are astounding. Derwent Water fills the lower portion of Borrowdale, and the lake is fed by streams filled with waterfalls. The dale constricts itself around the Jaws of Borrowdale, near the hamlet of Grange. Heading onwards, Borrowdale features interesting hamlets such as Rosthwaite, Stonethwaite, Seatoller and Seathwaite.

Borrowdale has an unfortunate claim to fame – that of supporting the highest rainfall in England. But in between the showers the air can be wonderfully clear for extended periods. If it does pour with rain, then remember the wealth of waterfalls and mount a search for some of them. There are four walks offered which explore the wonderful variety of landforms in the dale.

Ullscarf is a broad, whaleback rise of a fell. Its ascent is from Stonethwaite and the line used for the descent is via the wilderness dale of Langstrath. Seathwaite is the starting point for a walk over Green Gable and Great Gable, with the descent including a stretch of the celebrated smuggler's path called Moses Trod. Glaramara is an impressively bulky and knobbly fell, which is climbed purely for its own sake. It is like a range of fells in miniature, and the line of descent runs from Sty Head to Seatoller at the head of Borrowdale. The final walk is a shorter, easier affair, although it does include one short and steep ascent. Castle Crag is a wonderful little fell, not at all abashed by its lack of height, but standing proudly in the Jaws of Borrowdale and offering splendid views.

The "Borrowdale Bus" runs regularly from Keswick to Seatoller and walkers are urged to patronise this service. The car parks can become horribly crowded in the peak season and roadside parking is not only limited, but can be unsightly. There are plenty of accommodation options, from campsite and youth hostel, through farmhouse B&Bs, to the splendid Lodore Swiss Hotel. There are a handful of places offering food and drink, although these can be very crowded at busy times.

Anyone wanting to enquire further into the life and work of Borrowdale should head for the Seatoller Barn Visitor Centre. Displays there record industries and traditions as diverse as sheep-rearing and graphite mining.

Stanley Bond

Seatoller

10 Ullscarf

The broad and gently domed moorland summit of Ullscarf is in view from dozens of Lakeland Fells, but the eye passes it without much regard. It simply fails to attract attention. Strange that the fell should have been so fashioned, for it is surrounded by some ferocious looking crags, and any approach to the summit involves a difficult walk at some stage. The route offered here climbs Ullscarf from Stonethwaite in Borrowdale, although the fell could be climbed from a number of other places.

Distance: 7¹/₄ miles/12km	rugged ascent and descent, but broad and boggy on top.
Height gain: 2,130ft/650m	**Start/Finish:** Stonethwaite. GR263137.
Walking time: 5 hours	
Type of walk: Steep and	

Parking is extremely limited around the little hamlet of Stonethwaite. If staying at the campsite, Longthwaite Youth Hostel, or a nearby B&B, then car parking is provided at those places for patrons. The nearest alternative car park is at Seatoller, meaning that the walk would be longer as extra road walking would be included at the start and finish.

A narrow, dead end minor road runs into Stonethwaite, and a left turn in the hamlet reveals a track crossing Stonethwaite Beck. Turn left to follow a wall which accompanies the beck upstream, but walk this way for only a short while. Take the next turning to the left, where a path begins to climb up the fellside. This path zigzags up a steep and delightfully wooded slope, and there are fine views across the rugged, wooded reaches of Upper Borrowdale as height is gained.

Eventually, the path crosses over a hump of ground and proceeds across a rather knobbly patch of fell to reach the lonely pool of Dock Tarn. Walk south-east away from Dock Tarn, across rugged, boggy ground which features no clear path. Choose any line of ascent towards the distant dome of Ullscarf, outflanking areas of bog and deep heather on the lower parts of the fell.

As the ground steepens it becomes rockier, and there is a break of slope at Low Saddle, where a slight hump protrudes from the side of Ullscarf. It is worth pausing for a moment to enjoy the view along the length of Borrowdale towards Derwent Water. The walk from Low Saddle to the next hump at High Saddle is at a gentler gradient, and a simple slope of grass continues onwards towards the top of Ullscarf.

A notable feature of the summit of Ullscarf is the line of an old fence running across it. The posts offer a faultless guide across the higher slopes, and a cairn marks the summit at 2,370ft/726m. Ullscarf's central position in the Lake District assures the walker of a fine all-round view, although the high crest of the Helvellyn range bars the prospect further eastwards. The western panorama features more rugged fells, including Pillar, the Gables

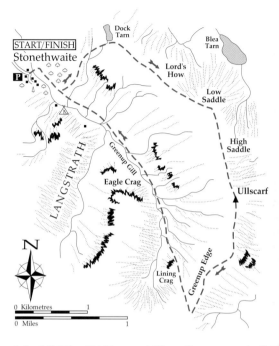

and Scafell Pike. Skiddaw and Blencathra appear to the north.

Continue following the course of the old fence to leave the broad moorland top of Ullscarf. The posts lead roughly southwards, with slight alterations, until turning more south-west. An area of rocky hummocks and boggy hollows is passed, and it is well to leave the line of the fence in some parts and outflank any squelchy areas.

As the route reaches the broad and boggy gap of

Greenup Edge, look for a path running off to the right. This runs down towards Greenup Gill and is a part of the celebrated Coast to Coast Walk. As the path is followed downhill, it passes close to Lining Crag and drops more steeply. The path is clear and obvious to follow, running parallel to Greenup Gill across a rugged fellside. The rocky prow of Eagle Crag towers high above to the left, frowning on walkers picking their way meekly beneath.

Little becks flowing into Greenup Gill are all crossed in turn, then a footbridge appears on the left spanning Greenup Gill. Don't cross this bridge, but continue downstream following the path alongside Stonethwaite Beck. This riverside path is also used by the Cumbria Way. A splendid little waterfall is passed and this is worth a moment of study. The path is then aligned to a wall running parallel to Stonethwaite Beck, running beneath the rugged, wooded fellside which was climbed in the early stages of the walk.

Simply look out for the left turn where a bridge crosses Stonethwaite Beck and a track leads back into the hamlet.

11 Great Gable

Borrowdale, Wasdale and Ennerdale could each claim Great Gable as their own fell, for it dominates the head of each dale. There are fine ascent routes from each of those dales. The short and steep ascent from Wasdale contrasts with the long walk-in necessary from Ennerdale, leaving the popular circuit from Borrowdale to be the route described here. There has been some path restoration on the approaches to this heavily used fell and there are also some steep and rocky scrambles to be negotiated.

Distance: 6 miles/10km	*fellwalk including steep*
Height gain:	*and rocky ascents and*
2,725ft/830m	*descents.*
Walking time: 4 hours	**Start/Finish:**
Type of walk: A tough	*Seathwaite. GR235123.*

Walk towards the farm at Seathwaite, noting that meals are sometimes available. There is often a prominent noticeboard displaying the number of dogs shot for sheep worrying – and dog walker should take note of this. Turn right to follow a walled track to a footbridge, and cross over the infant River Derwent.

The path climbs straight uphill alongside Sour Mill Gill, and this is probably one of the toughest way to start any Lakeland walk. The path has been reconstructed in many places, but at some point the use of hands are required to scramble up slabs and rock steps which could prove intimidating for more cautious walkers. If regular breaks are taken on the ascent, then it won't seem so bad, and there are fine views across the rugged dale head. Sour Milk Gill features some impressive waterfalls and has an interesting range of trees and shrubs which somehow cling to the steep and rocky ground.

When the steepest part of the climb comes to a close, a fellside wall is crossed and the path runs up into the hanging valley of Gillercomb. The course of Sour Milk Gill is still pursued upstream, but the path is often some distance away and uphill from the water. The climb out of Gillercomb is steep, but has no other difficulties. The steeper parts of the path have been reconstructed, and it is imperative that walkers stay on the path and do not cause unsightly erosion by trying to shortcut the zigzags.

A broad, grassy gap is reached between the fells of Base Brown and Green Gable. The path swings to the right to climb Green Gable. Simply follow it uphill. At a higher level, a prominent path runs in from the right and the way to the summit of Green Gable is well trodden. There is a cairn at 2,603ft/801m, and the most arresting feature is the rocky mass of Great Gable. Spend some time studying this awesome fell, because the walk has to get to the top of it. Further afield are more rugged fells, but their lines are softened by distance.

Descend on a path of pulverised rock from Green Gable to the rocky notch of Windy Gap. Looking up towards Great Gable could cause a crick in the neck but it is necessary to plot a course ahead, following paths where they exist, and looking for places where the bare rock has been worn smooth. Eventually, a cairned route crosses a broad boulderfield on top of Great Gable. The topmost point is a rock, and fixed on to it is a small bronze memorial in the shape of a relief model of the surrounding fells. This is a useful visual aid on a day when mist and drizzle swirl around the summit.

The altitude is 2,949ft/899m, and yet the view is practically blocked to the south by the rocky range of the Scafells. In other directions, there is an extensive vista, taking in practically all the most prominent Lakeland fells, as well as stretching towards southern Scotland and the Pennines. One of the most remarkable views is found away from the summit, by walking towards Wasdale Head for a few paces. The idea is to locate the Westmorland Cairn which is perched above the awesome crags and screes of the Napes. From there, a bird's eye view stretches along the length of Wasdale, looking across the remarkable jigsaw-like field pattern at the head of the dale.

The way off the summit on this particular walk is roughly south-west, picking up the path which descends to Beck Head. Taken steadily, this steep and rocky path is perfectly safe, but it is easy to start wrongly and end up being drawn down steep scree slopes.

Beck Head is the low slung gap between Great Gable and Kirk Fell. It is not necessary to land on the gap itself, but look out for a point where a path

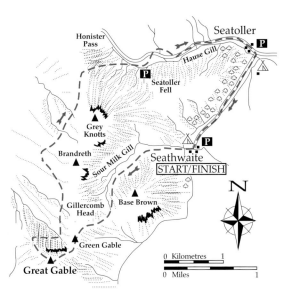

accompanied by a line of old iron fenceposts turns off to the right. This path is the celebrated Moses Trod – reputedly used by illicit spirit smugglers. Moses Trod cuts across the shoulders of Great Gable, crosses the headwaters of the River Liza, then cuts across the flanks of Green Gable.

Moses Trod is a fine route. It contours around the fellsides, or at least descends and climbs at gentle gradients. As the path crosses the slopes of Brandreth it is important not to be pulled off route along other paths on the slopes, but cut across the slopes of Grey Knotts to continue downhill. The path leads towards the eastern end of Fleetwith Pike, where a broad and obvious track is joined.

This track is the course of an old quarry tramway. By turning right it leads the walker straight down towards Honister Pass, where there are plenty of reminders of the heyday of slate quarrying. There is also a Youth Hostel sitting beside the road on the top of the pass. Turn right along a track below the youth hostel. This track runs parallel to the road, and so spares walkers having to tread the tarmac.

When the road has to be crossed, continue to look for traces of a parallel track, routed along the northern side of the road, and later pulling well away from the road. Don't worry, as a sudden turn to the right will lead straight down to Seatoller later. If a car is parked here, then the walk can end. Walkers relying on the Borrowdale Bus will also end here. Cars which have been parked at Seathwaite need to be retrieved by continuing the walk further, as follows.

Turn left on leaving the car park at Seatoller, then right along the minor road towards Seathwaite. The whole length of this road can be followed to the farm, or a footpath can be followed upstream from Seathwaite Bridge. Either way, look up the fellside to the right to spot the Borrowdale Yews and the spoil heaps of former graphite mines. The mines gave rise to a pencil industry, which still flourishes at Keswick even though local supplies of graphite have long been exhausted.

12 Glaramara

Glaramara is a splendidly romantic name for a fine fell, which somehow seems to suit its location in Upper Borrowdale. A day's walk over Glaramara includes rugged ridges, splendid views, aggressively rocky faces, waterfalls and the chance to enjoy a farmhouse tea at the end of it all. The walk could easily be extended beyond the switchback summit towards neighbouring fells, but Glaramara is a fine fell in its own right and it is best enjoyed at a leisurely pace for its own sake.

Distance: 10 miles/16km	fellwalk using fairly
Height gain:	obvious paths, but care
2,900ft/885m	needed in mist.
Walking time: 6 hours	**Start/Finish:** Seatoller.
Type of walk: A rugged	GR245137.

Starting from the car park at Seatoller, which is also the terminus for the Borrowdale Bus, walk down the road towards Rosthwaite for a while. The road crosses the River Derwent and there is immediately a turning on the right for Thornythwaite Farm. Walk only a short way along the access road and turn left to follow a path uphill alongside a wall. The slope becomes rugged and wooded, and the path later leads out on to an open fellside.

There is a small notice along the way which points

out the dangers of visiting Dove Nest Crag, but that is well away to the left and won't be approached. Instead, watch out for a path leading uphill to the right, climbing along the rugged ridge of Thornythwaite Fell. What might appear to be the summit of Glaramara ahead is the top of Comb Head – and this will become apparent as height is gained.

Once the initial steep slopes of Thornythwaite Fell begin to ease a little, the path crosses some rather squelchy ground. Watch for a divergence of paths at a later stage, because the left hand path includes a short climb up a rock step, while the right hand path manages to avoid this obstacle. Either way, the summit cairn on Glaramara is reached beyond at 2,560ft/783m. There are two summits of about equal height close together, but the one most walkers aim for is the northerly one, on account of its fine views.

Looking northwards from Glaramara, the eye is led along the verdant level meadows of Borrowdale, which are flanked by rugged, wooded slopes. Derwent Water and Skiddaw are seen beyond the Jaws of Borrowdale. In other directions there are many fine fells to be identified, and it is well to spot the top of Allen Crags because the walk is heading that way.

The whole crest of Glaramara is a switchback, featuring broad and stony humps and bumps, with occasional boggy areas and pools of water reflecting the sky. This is a crest to follow at a relaxed pace, taking time to deviate from the trodden path and look over the neighbouring dales. The final grassy hump of Allen Crags becomes stonier and features a rugged little summit with a cairn.

The view gradually becomes closed to the south as the bulky fells of Great End and Bow Fell loom above Allen Crags. The towering form of Great Gable is seen off to the right on approaching the summit, and the walk descends towards it in due course. First, there is a slight descent to the broad gap in the fells called Esk Hause. This is readily identifiable as there is a prominent cross-shaped stone shelter there.

Turn right to descend from Esk Hause, following a well trodden path downhill alongside Ruddy Gill. Don't be drawn down alongside the gill, but cross over a minor rise to pass the lovely Sprinkling Tarn. Attention is more likely to be drawn in the other direction, where the rocky buttresses and gullies of Great End brood dark and forbidding, seldom seeing sunlight. The path runs further downhill to land on the broad gap of Sty Head. It used to be said that if anyone sat there long enough, the whole world would pass by – and this may be true!

Turn right on Sty Head and follow the clear path across the foot of Great Gable to pass Styhead Tarn. This path has been completely reconstructed in places and it is essential that walkers follow it faithfully to avoid damaging the fellside. This route used to be seriously eroded, and much toil has been expended to stabilise the area. While work teams were restoring one eroded stretch, they came across the perfectly preserved, but

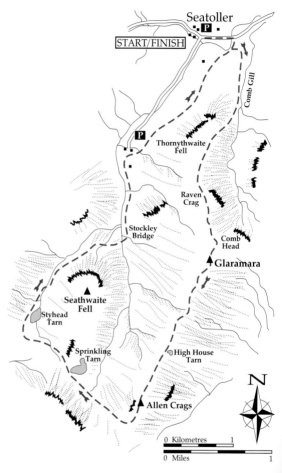

overgrown remains of an earlier packhorse route, so they promptly diverted their efforts on to the former route and incorporated it into their scheme.

Taylorgill Force lies off to the left in a deep and rocky gully, but trees prevent a clear view of it without a diversion being made. The path descends in zigzags to Stockley Bridge, which spans Grains Gill. Cross the bridge and turn left to follow a clear path and track to the farm buildings at Seathwaite.

While most walkers are content to follow the minor road straight back towards Seatoller, there are alternative valley paths which can be used. One heads off to the right of the farm buildings at Seathwaite and crosses the foot of the fells to reach Thornythwaite Farm. The other turns left to leave Seathwaite and crosses a bridge over the River Derwent, then turns right to follow the river downstream. This path rejoins the road to continue towards Seatoller.

13 Castle Crag

The Jaws of Borrowdale – a name to fire the imagination! This is the place where Borrowdale constricts itself, and the River Derwent squeezes between Castle Crag and Brund Fell. It is where rugged, wooded slopes frown on the huddled villages of Grange and Rosthwaite. Man has quarried the area, and yet failed to soften its contours. Castle Crag, although only a minor height, has a powerful personality and dominates the Jaws of Borrowdale. It is the centrepiece of this short and varied walk from Seatoller.

Distance: 6 miles/10km *and paths through woods*
Height gain: *and onto a steep and*
820ft/220m *rocky little fell.*
Walking time: 4 hours **Start/Finish:** *Seatoller.*
Type of walk: *Tracks* *GR245137.*

Leaving the back of the car park at Seatoller, there is a track leading towards Johnny's Wood. Bear right later to pass close to the Countrywide Holidays' Association Centre, which has a splendid view towards the head of Borrowdale. The path moves away from the centre, continuing through woodlands and following the course of the River Derwent downstream. Longthwaite Youth Hostel is reached further down the river, and the route follows its access road across a bridge. Turn left beside the next buildings and follow a field path towards the village of Rosthwaite.

Just as the path enters the village, look out for a left turn along a track which leads back towards the River Derwent. Follow the river a short way downstream, then cross over a hump-backed stone bridge. Turn right to continue downstream, following the path from the fields into the woods. Keep to the clearest paths in the woods, which skirt around the base of Castle Crag. There are a couple of old quarries, but don't enter them. Keep walking uphill, then downhill, to reach a broad bend in the River Derwent. A clear track is joined at this point, and there is a decision to be made.

The track is followed to the right until it leads out of the woods, continuing as a road to the village of Grange. This is a charming little settlement well worth exploring, and it features a fine old bridge spanning a very cobbly stretch of the River Derwent. There are also teas and snacks available. From the village, steps must be retraced to continue the walk over Castle Crag.

To omit Grange altogether, simply turn left to follow the track uphill from the river. This was once a fine highway in its time, but now it is simply a pleasant way up through the woods. The route soon emerges into a more open valley which is quite rugged. Castle Crag rises to the left, so steeply as to seem impregnable.

As the crag is passed, look out for a couple of paths on the left which make their way up the steep slopes of scree and slate spoil. The first path is fairly steep, and stays close to a rock face as it climbs. The second path is gentler and climbs a more stable, wooded slope. Both paths cross stiles on a fence before turning left to continue climbing. An engineered path makes its way up a steep slate spoil heap, emerging on a platform which features a stunning view across Upper Borrowdale. This is a place to stand and stare, where the steeply wooded slopes falling to the level meadows give a great sense of depth to the view.

Continuing uphill, there is a quarry to be passed, and this former industrial site is becoming delightfully overgrown. The summit of Castle Crag features a war memorial at 950ft/290m, as well as a crown of trees. There is another fine view, this time looking out of Borrowdale towards Derwent Water and the Skiddaw Fells. Despite Castle Crag's lack of height, the view is astoundingly varied. This is a great place from which to study the form of Borrowdale, from perhaps its most lovely stretch.

Carefully retrace steps downhill to return to the track in the rugged valley. Turn left to follow the track uphill and out across the fellside. A point is reached where paths for Seatoller and Scawdel part. Keep left and continue to contour around the rugged, brackeny fellside. A small stream is crossed while the route heads towards a gap straight ahead.

The path reaches a point where two small gates stand close together. Go through the gate on the left and follow a clear path downhill, which leads straight back to Seatoller. If the Seatoller Barn Visitor Centre is open, then it is well worth inspecting.

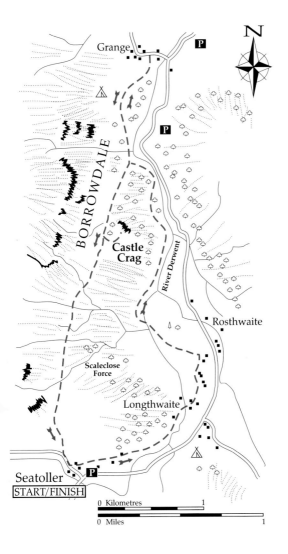

Grange

P

N

BORROWDALE

Castle
Crag

River Derwent

Rosthwaite

Scaleclose
Force

Longthwaite

Seatoller
START/FINISH

P

0 Kilometres 1

0 Miles 1

ENNERDALE

Ennerdale is one of the most remote and unfrequented of the Lakeland dales. Those who do penetrate its recesses are either keen explorers, or live in West Cumbria. There are those who cross its dale head on walks from Wasdale, Borrowdale and Buttermere, and some will take the trouble to stay at the remote Black Sail Hut Youth Hostel. The celebrated Coast to Coast Walk runs through Ennerdale on its way from St. Bees Head to Robin Hood's Bay, with a high-level trek along the High Stile range offered for keen fellwalkers with stamina.

Cars are not allowed beyond the Bowness Knott Car Park, close to the shore of Ennerdale Water. The middle parts of the dale are reserved for forestry vehicles and farm vehicles running to and from Gillerthwaite. There is a waymarked forest trail known as the Nine Becks Walk, but this features few views.

The two walks described in this section break free of the coniferous gloom and enjoy fine views around the dale. The walks are very different. One is a fairly easy circuit around the shore of Ennerdale Water. The lake shore can be quite rugged in places, so this is no simple stroll. Views along the length of the dale or across the lake are often charming. The other walk is a more strenuous fellwalk which covers the summits of Haycock, Scoat Fell and Steeple. Views across the dale are more extensive because of the great height gained. Steeple is a fine name for a fine fell. It appears as a knife-edge blade of rock, but proves quite straightforward to climb.

There are few facilities in Ennerdale. The two Youth Hostels in the dale are generally regarded as being off the beaten track. Other accommodation down-dale is sparse, and apart from the Hare and Hounds at Ennerdale Bridge, you would have to travel far to get any food and drink. There is only an occasional bus service to Ennerdale Bridge, so this remains a place where visitors either have to drive or walk in to enjoy the solitude of the place.

The roe buck

Christine Isherwood

Old walkers and fishermen will be able to recall the Anglers' Hotel, which was demolished when the level of Ennerdale Water was raised slightly. Even older walkers will be able to recall the dale before it was cloaked in alien spruce and fir, but the time is fast approaching when everyone will remember Ennerdale as a forested dale.

14 Ennerdale Water

*Ennerdale is one of Lakeland's most inaccessible dales.
There are three reasons for this. First, it is well to the
west, where approaches are generally not made by most
visitors. Second, it is served only by a forest road and
vehicles cannot proceed far along it without a permit.
Third, there is no public transport to the dale. Those who
would walk in Ennerdale must park their cars below the
rugged prow of Bowness Knott. This is well situated for
a walk which makes a complete circuit around the shores
of Ennerdale Water.*

Distance:
7 miles/11km
Height gain:
490ft/150m
Walking time: 3¹/₂
hours
Type of walk: A

*lakeshore walk including
forest tracks and fellside
paths, rugged in one
part.*
Start/Finish: *Bowness
Knott Car Park.
GR109154.*

---

*Driving to Ennerdale means using roads which become
progessively narrower, twisting and turning as they
approach the dale. Sometimes, they appear to veer away
from the dale, which is occasionally seen along the way.
Eventually, the Bowness Knott car park is reached and it
is important that this facility be used. There is a toilet
block and an information board showing the layout of
various waymarked walking routes in Ennerdale Forest.
Anyone trying to drive further into Ennerdale will be*

confronted by a very sternly worded notice forbidding further access and outlining the bye-laws being infringed and the penalties for their infringement!

Proceed from the Bowness Knott car park, following the forest road into Ennerdale. This gradually slopes down towards the lake shore, providing an easy start and allowing walkers to get into their stride. There are views towards some of the higher fells, although these will be seen to better advantage as the walk continues. The forested slopes rising to the left finally expire on the rugged slopes of Great Borne, which can't be seen from this side of the lake. The forest road passes the head of Ennerdale Water, where boggy ground has been formed on top of the sands and gravels brought into the lake by the River Liza.

Turn right after passing the levels at the head of the lake and cross the River Liza using a bridge. Gradually bear to the right along a path which reaches the foot of the fellside on the opposite side of the dale. Forest plantations give way to a more natural covering of trees. Study these carefully, as here are some stunted sessile oaks which are thought to be remnants of the ancient Lakeland forest cover. Only because of their relative inaccessibilty and poor worth as timber have they been spared the axe.

As the path runs along the shores of Ennerdale Water, there are opportunities to look back across the lake towards Bowness Knott and the huge rock and heather shoulders supporting Great Borne. Looking ahead, the rugged prow of Anglers' Crag can be seen dipping its foot into the waters of the lake. Cautious walkers might wonder if they will be able to get around it. The best course to take is over the little gap which will be noticed at a higher level. Make sure that the path is taken which leads up towards this gap, so that steep, rugged ground doesn't have to be climbed at the last minute.

Once this gap is reached, there is a finer prospect across the lake on account of the extra height gained. There is an opportunity to look towards the fells around the head of Ennerdale, though these can be studied more easily from the foot of the lake. Follow the path down from the gap towards level ground where the River Ehen leaves the lake. There is a bridge across the river just below a weir. The weir was put in place to raise the lake level slightly; in effect converting the lake into a reservoir. Water is drawn off, along with more from Wast Water, to be used as a coolant at the Sellafield nuclear power station. Water which isn' taken also reaches Sellafield, as the River Ehen enters the Irish Sea at that point.

After crossing the bridge, continue along the lakeshore path, which is fringed with woodlands hedges and fields. Views along the length of the lake take in Ennerdale's most notable fells – Steeple and Pillar. The latter fell displays the monstrous tower of rock from which it originally took its name. The raising of the level of Ennerdale Water led to the loss of one of Lakeland's most notable hostelries – the Anglers' Hotel. A more drastic proposal to raise the level of the lake even further was defeated in the 1980s.

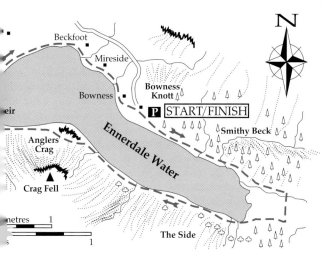

All that remains is to complete the lakeshore path around the broad foot of the lake. The rugged prow of Bowness Knott ends where Bowness Point drops into the lake, and so it is easy to gauge where the walk is going to end. It is possible to head uphill to the left as soon as Bowness Point is reached, and this returns walkers directly to the car park. Alternatively, to squeeze a little more distance from this lakeshore circuit, continue around the foot of Bowness Point to the forest road further along. A sharp left turn leads back up the forest road to the car park at Bowness Knott.

15 Steeple

Steeple is properly an Ennerdale fell, although most people who visit its summit tend to do so on walks from Wasdale. This walk, however, starts in Ennerdale and includes the whole of Steeple's noble ridge. It is not climbed in isolation, but coupled with neighbouring Haycock – a fell whose domed, stony summit is less trodden than many of its illustrious neighbours in both Ennerdale and Wasdale. Haycock and Steeple together offer a fine fellwalking circuit, and the ridges running to them from Ennerdale are unlikely to be crowded with walkers.

Distance:
10¼ miles/17km
Height gain:
2,790ft/850m
Walking time: 7 hours
Type of walk:
Fellwalking, with tracks, paths, pathless terrain, as well as rugged ground.
Start/Finish: Bowness Knott Car Park.
GR109154.

Traffic in Ennerdale is restricted, and visitors can proceed no further than the Bowness Knott car park.

Walk along the road leaving the car park penetrating further into Ennerdale. The road runs close to Ennerdale Water, and there are tantalising glimpses of fine fells. Watch out for a turning on the right and cross a bridge over the River Liza.

Walk across the flat dale-bottom towards the forested dale of Woundell, which gives access to the higher fells beyond. Woundell Beck is formed from the confluence of Deep Gill and Silvercove Beck. There is a footbridge over the latter, after which a right turn leads up through a small patch of forest on the fellside spur between the two becks. Simply continue up the path on to the open fell, and aim to follow the broad ridge further uphill.

The ridge rises between Silver Cove and Great Cove, two lonely little dale-heads which must be among the least-visited places in the Lake District. Even so, there are vague signs of habitation and industry even in these remote enclaves. A small mine might be spotted by carefully scouring Silver Cove with the eye, but the walker would need to be deep within Deep Gill to spot the remains of a building constructed against an outcrop of rock. The heathery ridge gradually becomes more grassy and climbs at a gentler gradient, then there is steeper, rockier ground before the route gains the crest of the higher fells.

There is a fine drystone wall running across the broad gap between Caw Fell and Haycock. Turn left to follow this wall towards Haycock. The rocky excrescence of Little Gowder Crag is no real problem, and the wall has been built all the way up its slopes. Haycock's broad and stony dome rises beyond. There are two cairns on the summit – one on either side of the wall, so that whichever way the fell is climbed a cairn will be reached at 2,618ft/798m.

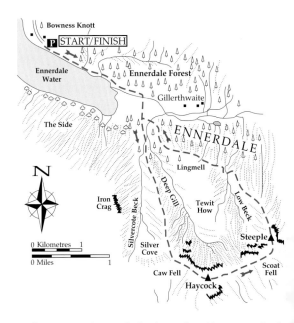

Walkers expecting to look along the ridge towards the summits of Pillar and Great Gable will be disappointed to find that Scoat Fell largely blocks the view in that direction. The Scafell range is well displayed across Wasdale. Looking across Ennerdale, the flanks of the High Stile range seem bare and less impressive than when viewed from across Buttermere. Fells such as Skiddaw, Helvellyn and Black Combe feature more distantly, while the whaleback hump of the Isle of Man might be spotted in the Irish Sea on a clear day.

Continue following the wall down from the summit of Haycock. Stony ground runs practically down to the next gap, then a grassier crest rises towards Scoat Fell. The grassy crest levels out before a rockier slope leads on to the summit at 2,760ft/843m. Pillar now features much more prominently in the view, as it is the next fell in line along this rugged ridge. This walk, however, descends back into Ennerdale via Steeple – a fell which might not yet have been noticed by some walkers, who should now look for it from the northern side of the fell.

Steeple is revealed as a sharp blade of rock rising between Mirk Cove and Mirklin Cove. If it was being climbed from Ennerdale, it would offer steep, rugged and unremitting slopes. Climbing it from Scoat Fell, however, is relatively easy. There is only a rugged little gap separating the two fells, and this is easily crossed by walkers who take care where they plant their feet. From the lowest point of the gap to the summit of Steeple, the ascent is less than 70ft/20m. The summit is an airy perch at 2,687ft/819m.

Views are restricted by the bulk of Scoat Fell and Pillar, yet some of the higher parts of the Gables and Scafell range can be seen through a gap. It is the nearer prospects which should be studied more closely. Here craggy slopes plunge into Mirk Cove and Mirklin Cove, where walkers seldom tread.

The steep and rocky slopes on both sides of Steeple's summit channel walkers on to a northerly descent. The ground falls towards Ennerdale, being steep at first, then the gradient eases for a while, before steepening again. It might be tempting to head straight downhill into Ennerdale but this should be resisted. Drift to the left towards Low Beck and cross it using a clear path.

The path leaves Low Beck and cuts across the fellside well above the forest-line. Boggy ground is crossed on the minor hump of Lingmell, before the path begins to drift downhill. The path was accommodated on an unplanted strip of fellside when the rest of Ennerdale was swathed in coniferous plantations, and as the ground steepens the path leads straight downhill to land on a forest track in the dale-bottom.

Turn left along the forest track, which crosses Woundell Beck. This beck was encountered earlier during the day, and a right turn leads along a path which was used at the start of the walk. Cross the bridge over the River Liza to link with the main forest road through Ennerdale. A left turn along this road leads along the shores of Ennerdale Water, ending with a short climb uphill to return to the Bowness Knott Car Park.

WASDALE

Wasdale is perhaps the most dramatic dale in the Lake District. Its dale head skyline is used as the Lake District National Park logo. Largely treeless, Wasdale presents everything to the visitor at a glance, leaving only a few folds to be discovered by walkers prepared to explore the fells. Here are ranged some of the highest mountains in England, as well as the deepest lake. Great scree slopes observed falling into dark Wast Water, or down the flanks of Great Gable and the Scafells, lead some walkers to believe that walking in Wasdale is going to be dangerous. It could be, but it just needs care.

Three walks are described along the length of Wasdale, taking in a variety of fine fells. Some are well known, the others comparatively little known. Even the Wastwater Screes, which look so intimidating from afar, prove rather more amenable on closer acquaintance. The walk along the foot of the Wastwater Screes is tied with a high-level walk above them afterwards.

The Mosedale Horseshoe is one of the classic horseshoe walks of the Lake District. Walkers can decide whether or not to include Kirk Fell and Yewbarrow, but they should certainly include Pillar, Scoat Fell and Red Pike. On the ascent to Pillar, the High Level Route is the most entertaining and dramatic approach. England's highest mountain – Scafell Pike – can be climbed from Wasdale Head using Lingmell as a mighty stepping stone. The descent can be accomplished by way of the dramatic Corridor Route, before using an old packhorse way to return to Wasdale Head.

Accommodation, food and drink are limited in Wasdale. It is often a good idea to book accommodation well in advance, although chances could be taken with farmhouse teas and bar meals if the queues aren't too long. Public transport is absent, although in the past minibus services have been run to Wasdale Head. Hardy fellwalkers could use transport services in other dales, such as Borrowdale, Eskdale or Buttermere, then walk over the high passes to reach Wasdale and settle down somewhere to enjoy a few fine walks. One surprising facility at Wasdale Head is the Barn Door Climbing Shop, close to the Wasdale Head Inn. This enables walkers who have forgotten, lost or broken any key items of equipment to obtain replacements and continue their explorations without a break.

16 Wast Water Screes

There must be many casual visitors to Wasdale who look across the lake at the Wast Water Screes and are awe-struck at the sight. Shattered black buttresses of rock have been riven with dark gullies which spew vast fans of bouldery scree into the dark waters of the lake. Some imagine that walking there must be impossible, then they notice the thin path above the water-line, and see an occasional walker picking a way along it. Improbable, but not impossible; it is a fine walk above and below the Wast Water Screes.

Distance: 9 miles/15km
Height gain:
1,970ft/600m
Walking time: 5 hours
Type of walk: A
bouldery lakeshore path

followed by moderate
upland fellwalking.
Start/Finish: Near the
National Trust Campsite,
Wasdale Head.
GR183075.

Parking is available near the National Trust campsite at Wasdale Head. Park after turning off the narrow road at the head of Wast Water, then continue on foot across a bridge spanning Lingmell Gill. Note the smooth, rounded boulders in the stream bed, which tell of the volume of water when the beck is in spate. Turn right along the access track towards Wasdale Head Hall Farm.

The access track runs along the shore of Wast Water

for a short while, before turning towards the farm. Don't walk to the farm, but continue along the shoreline path, eventually leaving the enclosed pastures near the farm. The path rises slightly above the shore, and the slopes falling from the fells towards the lake are rugged, but not yet spectacular. The walk is quite easy as the path is reasonably well surfaced and simply contours across the rugged fellside without getting involved with the vegetation.

Later, the path begins to cross some of the fans of scree. Some walkers begin to tread gingerly and speak in hushed voices, imagining that one step out of line will bring the entire stony slope sliding inexorably into the lake. Be assured that it won't happen, but all the same, if a boulder comes crashing down from the broken crags above, it would be advisable to step out of its way!

The scree slope suddenly changes from being composed of gravel and cobbles into an altogether more chaotic arrangement of boulders. Some of these boulders are simply enormous, and lie slumbering in drunken postures with their roots deep in the slope. The path becomes a more patchy affair, and eventually hands have to be brought into play to grapple a way past some of the rocks. Progress may well slow down to a crawl, and the prospect ahead may not look too good at times, but all the difficulties end suddenly.

Continue along the scree path and cross a rugged slope to reach the foot of Wast Water. A little building with an access track is found here, and walkers can enjoy a short, easy stroll for a moment.

Wast Water looks natural, but it is used as a reservoir. Water is pumped away to Sellafield, where it is used as a coolant at the nuclear power plant along with additional supplies from Ennerdale Water. Wast Water is also notable for being the deepest lake in the Lake District. Its surface altitude of 200ft/61m and great depth of 258ft/79m means that its lowest point is 58ft/18m below sea level.

Don't go through the first gate reached on the track, but turn left and start climbing uphill alongside a wall. This wall reaches the tremendous cleft of Greathall Gill. Do not cross the gill, but start climbing uphill alongside it. The slope is rough and relentlessly steep, but it does ease slightly as height is gained. If excuses for occasional rests are required, the view across to Buckbarrow and Seatallan is improving all the time. The brackeny lower slopes give way to grassier slopes above, and eventually the crest of the fell is reached and other paths are joined.

Turn left to walk up any of the parallel paths which have been blazed up the slopes of Whin Rigg. They are all basically going the same way. Look out for the summit cairn at 1,755ft/536m, and pause to enjoy the view across Wasdale. By teetering on the brink of the cliffs, there is a fine sense of space and the shores of Wast Water only recently traversed can be observed from this height. Further afield here are fine fells in view, ranged all around Wasdale, but including other groups such as the Coniston Fells and Black Combe.

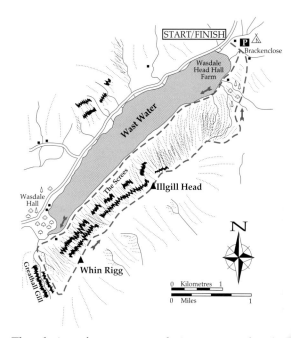

The choice of route onwards is a matter for the individual. There are those who would prefer to stay on the clearest path and head across the broad dip before climbing on to Illgill Head. Others will make the most of the views from the cliff edges and wander around the heads of gullies and perch on prows of rock to sample the best views of the Wastwater Screes fanning out towards the lake.

Either way, Illgill Head is the next summit in line and a gradual, grassy ascent leads to the summit cairn at 1,983ft/609m. The view towards Wasdale Head improves, and the fine lines of the fells around the dale-head soar skywards, completely dwarfing the tiny hamlet scattered among the jigsaw-piece fields. The Wasdale Head Inn is easily spotted as it is the largest building, painted white, and has the word "INN" on the nearest gable. Wast Water is best appreciated by walking towards the edge of the fell.

The descent from Illgill Head is made by walking roughly north-eastwards down a slope which gradually steepens. There are a couple of paths which might be used, and both head towards a broad gap in the fells. The vegetation underfoot changes from grass to heather and bracken. By keeping to the left, a clear path will be joined which runs straight across a rugged slope as it descends towards Wasdale. A stand of trees is passed and a drystone wall accompanies the track downhill. The Fell & Rock Club hut is passed at Brackenclose, where a left turn leads back towards the National Trust campsite and car park.

17 Pillar

From Wasdale Head, Pillar looks anything but a pillar. Its broad, stony dome rises above the head of Mosedale and is flanked by Red Pike, Scoat Fell and Kirk Fell. It is necessary to go on to the Ennerdale slopes of the fell to discover how the fell got its name, for that is where the monstrous monolith of Pillar Rock is to be found. This walk is basically the celebrated Mosedale Horseshoe – a classic Lakeland circuit. There are all sorts of ways the circuit can be shortened or lengthened, depending on the energy of the walker.

Distance:
10¼ miles/17km
Height gain:
3,250ft/990m
Walking time: 6 hours
Type of walk:
Fellwalking, including

good tracks and paths as well as very rocky terrain.
Start/Finish: The Green, Wasdale Head.
GR187085.

The road running to Wasdale Head reaches a dead end either at the Wasdale Head Inn or Burnthwaite Farm. Cars can be parked at The Green, which is where the final road junction is located at the dale head. The Green is a triangular area of grass next to an old schoolhouse. Walk along the last stretch of the road to the Wasdale Head Inn, and continue around the side of the building. A track leads towards an attractive hump-backed stone footbridge. Don't cross this bridge, but keep to the track, which seems to aim straight for the steep slopes of Kirk Fell.

As the path rises to a fellside gate, there is a turning off to the left, so that Kirk Fell no longer looms overhead. Instead, there is a clear path which even descends slightly as it works its way around the foot of Kirk Fell. A lot of work has been accomplished on this path, which was once quite badly worn in places. There are a couple of small streams to be crossed, where the path has been cobbled right through the water.

Mosedale is a popular name among Lakeland dales, and they are all boggy-floored and consequently uninhabited. After wandering alongside Mosedale, the path begins to climb up the flanks of Kirk Fell, and crosses Gatherstone Beck. The gradient steepens, but there are zigzags to offset this, and the path continues plainly towards Black Sail Pass – the broad gap in between Kirk Fell and Pillar. Turn left on top of the pass, following another path up the blunt and grassy ridge leading up towards Pillar. This shoulder of the fell is known as Looking Stead, and beyond its summit there is a choice of paths.

While it is possible to reach the summit of Pillar simply by climbing higher and higher, there is also a spectacularly rocky alternative route which can be completed with a little extra effort. It is known as the High Level Route, and branches off to the right from the other ridge path just beyond the minor summit of Looking Stead. The High Level

Route contours around the rugged slopes of Green Cove and crosses a dip before rising towards a prominent cairn. This is Robinson's Cairn, from which there is a view of Pillar Rock rising almost vertically from the flanks of Pillar. It has three distinct peaks – High Man, Low Man and Pisgah. The deep cleft between Pisgah and High Man is known as Jordan Gap.

The path is clearly trodden beyond Robinson Cairn, despite the forbiddingly rocky nature of the fellside. Crossing bouldery ground, the walker is suddenly confronted with a steep, rocky ramp having a cliff both above and below it. This is the Shamrock Traverse, and it proves not nearly so difficult as it might first appear. Beyond the traverse is more rocky ground which leads to the gap between Pisgah and Pillar. Pisgah can be ascended by a short and easy scramble on bare rock, but to reach the top of Pillar Rock requires serious scrambling which, if attempted, must be protected with the use of a rope and appropriate belays.

To continue with the walk, climb straight up the rocky flank of Pillar following a well worn path. By degrees, height is gained and soon there is a view which is level with the top of Pillar Rock. As more height is gained the rock seems to dwindle in stature and thoughts turn towards the summit of Pillar itself. After all the excitement of the High Level Route, the top of Pillar turns out to be broad and stony, with a trig point and sundry cairns. The altitude is a lofty 2,927ft/853m and views are splendid in clear weather. The Scafell range and

Pillar Rock

Pillar

Robinson
Cairn

Looking
Stead

Wind
Gap

Black Sail Pass

Red
Pike

M O S E D A L E

Scoat
Tarn

Dore
Head

Stirrup
Crag

Mosedale Beck

Low Tarn

Wasdale
Head

P

START/FINISH

Yewbarrow

Down in
the Dale

P

Dropping
Crag

Bowderdale

Brackenclose

Wast Water

0 Kilometres 1

0 Miles 1

N

99

Great Gable look especially fine, while most other fells of note can also be identified, including the Helvellyn and Skiddaw ranges in the far distance.

Descend south-westwards from the summit of Pillar, following a path steeply down a stony slope to reach the narrow, rocky cleft of Wind Gap. The configuration of fells and dales around this gap ensures that there will almost always be some sort of air movement – hence the name. Climbing up the rocky slope from Wind Gap, the broad and bouldery summit of Scoat Fell is gained, and it is best to keep to the left side of a stone wall which runs across the first rocky summit. The true summit of Scoat Fell is a short way beyond, rising to 2,760ft/843m. It is up to each individual walker whether or not to go all the way to the summit, as there is a path bearing off to the left beforehand which allows the summit to be omitted altogether.

The Mosedale Horseshoe walk continues by heading for the summit of Red Pike, which lie roughly south-east of Scoat Fell. There is only a broad and fairly gentle dip between the two summits, and Red Pike features a rather narrower crest rising to 2,707ft/828m. The broad crest of Scoat Fell and the huge bulk of Pillar have the effect of concealing half of the view, so that the walker is forced to observe the Scafell, Gable and Helvellyn ranges, as well as more distant features further southwards.

Continuing roughly southwards along the crest of Red Pike, the ground begins to fall away more steeply and there is a gradual drift south-east as the path approaches the gap of Dore Head. In previous decades, the Mosedale Horseshoe was generally rounded off with a rapid scree-run descent into Mosedale. Unfortunately, the screes have been torn off the fellside, leaving an unsightly scar and this descent cannot be recommended. Yewbarrow could be added as an "extra" fell, but it requires a steep and rocky ascent, involving the use of hands, followed by a long and steep descent which is tough on the knees. Some parts of Yewbarrow are also becoming badly eroded, so the fell is omitted from this route description.

The gentlest descent is parallel to Over Beck across the lower slopes of Yewbarrow. Make sure that this path is followed carefully, so that great depths of bracken aren't encountered at a lower level. The path runs beneath the prow of Dropping Crag, then cuts across the fellside to reach a wall. There is a much clearer path running downhill alongside the wall, frowned upon by the ferocious crags of Bell Rib. Cross the wall towards its end and swing sharply left to follow a path sloping gradually down towards the road. Note, this is not the path which drops directly towards the road, although it doesn't really matter which one is taken. When the road is reached, turn left and follow it back towards Wasdale Head to reach the triangular green where the walk started.

18 Scafell Pike

Scafell Pike is not only the highest mountain in the Lake District, but as a consequence it is also the highest mountain in England. As befits a mountain bearing such an accolade, it is rugged from head to foot, offering plenty of tough ascents and descents. The location of Scafell Pike allows ascents to be made from dales as widely spread as Eskdale, Langdale or Borrowdale, but the ascent described here is from Wasdale. Lingmell is used as an enormous stepping stone to the summit and the Corridor Route is followed on the descent.

Distance:
8 miles/13km
Height gain:
3,150ft/960m
Walking time: 5 hours
Type of walk: Classic

fellwalking on fairly clear paths across steep and rocky terrain.
Start/Finish: The Green, Wasdale Head. GR187085.

Park on the triangular grassy green at Wasdale Head, where the road branches to serve Wasdale Head Inn and Burnthwaite Farm. Walk a short way back down the road from The Green, and take a field path off to the left. This crosses the level dale bottom and seems to aim straight towards the steep and rugged flanks of Lingmell. The path passes areas of scrub and crosses Lingmell Beck using a footbridge.

Turn right after crossing the footbridge. There is a wall slanting up across the fellside and enough walkers have followed its course to leave a path alongside. However, the path really cuts across the fellside at a lesser gradient within the area enclosed by the wall. By staying on the true footpath, the blunt ridge of Lingmell is reached at a lower point, and by turning left to walk uphill the wall is crossed using a ladder stile. Anyone following the course of the wall uphill will not use the ladder stile.

The blunt ridge is steep and walkers may need to pause for breath from time to time. In doing so, the unfolding panorama can be observed, both across the lower parts of Wasdale and up towards the summit of Scafell Pike. There is later an easing of the gradient, and the broad, grassy shoulder of Lingmell is then crossed by a ruined wall. It is possible to follow the wall off to the right and so reach the gap in between Lingmell and Scafell Pike. However, it is also worth climbing to the summit of Lingmell, even though this means ascending a rugged, stony slope.

Lingmell is ideally positioned for viewing Great Gable, as the eye can scan the face of the fell from top to bottom, taking in all the detail of its rocky ridges and slopes of scree. It is also possible to peer into Piers Gill – a dramatic, rocky cleft cut into the lower slopes of Lingmell.

Scafell Pike dominates the view to the south, and by heading in its direction a gap and a ruined wall are crossed. A short climb uphill links with a path which twists and turns as it negotiates a steep and bouldery slope. Stay on the path – such as it is – and in mist take note of the cairns which have been erected along its course. The summit of Scafell Pike is unlikely to be in doubt, as it is crowned with a huge platform cairn with the trig point off to one side. The altitude is a supreme 3,206ft/977m.

Every notable Lakeland fell is in view, but the eye is first drawn to the ferocious face of neighbouring Scafell. By degrees, the vista widens beyond Great Gable to the other Wasdale fells, past the Buttermere fells to the more distant Skiddaw fells. Blencathra and the Helvellyn range are backed by the more distant Pennines, which can be seen stretching beyond the Langdale Pikes, too. The Coniston Fells peter out towards Morecambe Bay and the Duddon Estuary, before Black Combe raises its sprawling shoulders. And so back to Scafell. In clear weather the Isle of Man might be seen, as well as parts of southern Scotland, and even North Wales. It is a comprehensive view which always springs surprises as weather conditions allow for variations.

In clear weather identify Broad Crag and head towards it. In mist, play safe and take a compass bearing, as the mass of boulders which make up the summit of Scafell Pike can seem very confusing and each of the cairned paths looks very much like the others. The path towards Broad Crag drops down steeply to a rocky gap, and at that point a left turn should be made to continue downhill. Note that this course leads unerringly into Piers Gill – where no walker should proceed – so be sure to turn right along the clear path which is reached before the rock walls of the gill begin to close in.

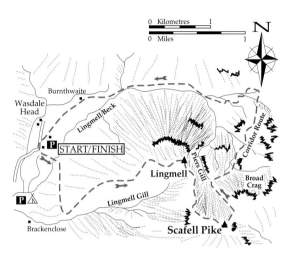

The clearest path across the fellside is known as the Corridor Route; in decades past it was referred to as the "Guides Route" and was used by mountain guides operating from Borrowdale. Follow this path wherever it leads, across the bouldery fellside, or across streams, or even across a bar of rock which seems to bring progress to a halt. Hands will need to be used briefly while crossing this bar, then the path becomes plain again. The Corridor Route makes a rather messy crossing of Skew Gill before the final run towards Styhead Pass. Note that there is no need to go as far as Sty Head. There is a rather more pleasant descent into Wasdale which is available.

Look out for a grassy path zigzagging down from Sty Head which keeps well below the usual stony path across the flanks of Great Gable. This zigzag path is the former packhorse way and it is a joy to use. It leads downhill and crosses a couple of streams, most notably crossing a stream just before a confluence with Lingmell Beck, which issues from the lower end of the great gash of Piers Gill. The fells tower high overhead on the way down towards the lower pastures of Wasdale. The path running roughly parallel to Lingmell Beck joins the stony path which cuts across the face of Great Gable. Stone walls channel the path towards Burnthwaite Farm, and the farm access road allows a direct return towards The Green.

The walled lane runs through fields which have impressively thick, irregular walls which were created when the dale head was cleared of rocks to make pasture land. The little church of St. Olaf can be visited, which is reputed to be England's smallest church (at the foot of England's highest mountain, close to England's deepest lake).

ESKDALE

Eskdale may lack a major lake, and indeed even lacks a major settlement, but it abounds in charm and interest. Threaded by a bright river which is accompanied by a miniature railway, the dale has many hidden secrets which only walkers are capable of discovering. Fine waterfalls tumble down gorges hidden behind screens of trees, and mouldering old iron mines and quarries have likewise been softened by greenery.

Eskdale provides a challenging approach to many travellers. They either drive all the way around the perimeter of the Lake District before heading into the dale, or they take a chance on the gruesome gradients and hairy hairpins of the Wrynose and Hardknott Passes. There is no main road running near the dale. Few travellers realise that there is good rail access via the Cumbria Coast Line and the Ravenglass & Eskdale Railway. Despite the latter line being a miniature affair, with lovely little steam and diesel engines, it is not simply there for tourists, but is a legitimate public transport service along the length of the dale. The railway has little halts at intervals, as well as its own cafes, museum and pub!

Once Eskdale has been reached, there are plenty of facilities, even if there is no major town or even village to house them all. There are hotels, pubs, B&Bs, a youth hostel and campsite. Items of interest and curiosity abound, including a restored cornmill at Boot, the grave of the master foxhunter

Tommy Dobson at St. Catherine's Church, Hardknott Roman Fort and the lovely hidden waterfall of Stanley Force. In the past, there was commerce between Eskdale and Wasdale on a route known as the Corpse Road, as bodies were occasionally carried along it for burial.

Although there are only two walks in this section, they take in a wide variety of scenery and terrain. Lofty Scafell can be climbed towards the head of Eskdale using a fairly well graded ascent. The descent is more rugged, featuring plenty of rocky buttresses and later some lovely waterfalls. Hardknott Fort was constructed in a commanding dale head position by the Romans, and a walk from that point can take in the adjacent fell of Hard Knott. Again there is a chance to look at some fine waterfalls in Lingcove Beck on the descent.

19 Scafell

There are many ways for a fellwalker to bring Scafell underfoot. Some of the approach routes are long and tedious, while others are seriously rocky and verge upon rock-climbing. The Terrace Route from Eskdale is relatively easy, or at any rate free of technical difficulty, and it conveys walkers to the summit of Scafell in stages which are in themselves interesting. A descent from the summit can be made between rugged, rocky slopes, and providing walkers take this slowly and steadily there should be no cause for concern.

Distance:	gradual ascent, a steeper,
10¼ miles/17km	rockier descent and some
Height gain:	bog.
2,950ft/900m	**Start/Finish:** Wha
Walking time: 6 hours	House, Eskdale.
Type of walk:	GR201009.
Fellwalking, with a	

To start the walk, cross the stile on the opposite side of the road to Wha House Farm and follow the path uphill. The path passes through a sheepfold as it leaves the enclosed rough pastures, then a drystone wall is followed further uphill. The Terrace Route drifts away from the wall and crosses a wilderness fellside of rock, bog, heather and a few rowan trees. Keep an eye on the path, which is plain to see, but if it is lost to sight it might be difficult to discover again. There are a few cairns which help to keep walkers on course across hummocky ground. After crossing Catcove Beck, the path begins to climb towards Slight Side, becoming steeper as height is gained.

Continuing from Slight Side, cross a gentle dip and start climbing gradually uphill again. The first slope is relatively short and soon gives way to the shoulder of Long Green, which is a good stance from which to view Scafell Pike's craggy flanks. One final stony slope suddenly gives way to the summit cairn on Scafell at 3,162ft/964m.

As might be expected, the higher mass of Scafell Pike blocks the view of some distant fells, with only small portions of the Helvellyn and Langdale fells in view, although many other prominent heights can be seen. Seaward, parts of southern Scotland and the Isle of Man can be seen on a clear day. Long stretches of the Cumbria and Lancashire coastlines support the feeling of being on the fringes of Lakeland, with lordly Scafell Pike dominating half of the view and the hills in the opposite direction dwindling rapidly towards sea level.

In clear weather there should be no problem locating the line of descent, but in mist it needs to be searched for with care, as it is too easy for walkers to be drawn onto the dangerous slopes and buttresses of Scafell Crag. Leave the summit cairn and walk roughly northwards for about 100yds/m, to a stony depression. Turn right to pick up the line of a path running downhill. This path quickly steepens and has been completely reconstructed to avoid further erosion to the bowl

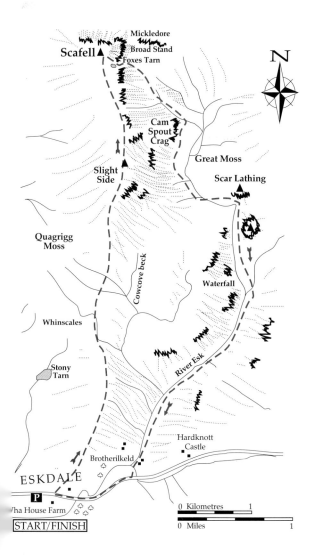

Mickledore
Broad Stand
Scafell ▲
Foxes Tarn

Cam
Spout
Crag

Great Moss

Scar Lathing

Slight
Side

Quagrigg
Moss

Cowcove beck

Waterfall

Whinscales

Stony
Tarn

River Esk

Hardknott
Castle

Brotherilkeld

ESKDALE

P

Wha House Farm

START/FINISH

N

0   Kilometres   1

0   Miles   1

of scree surrounding Foxes Tarn. The tarn is a mere puddle, but spotting it confirms that the walker is still on course. Continuing downhill from Foxes Tarn, pick a way gingerly down a dark and damp rocky gully. Conditions underfoot are uneven, but there are enough good footholds for it to be treated like a staircase. The gully debouches on to bouldery scree between Scafell and Scafell Pike.

Continue downhill on the bouldery scree, where the hollow it occupies is later used by a stream, that breaks into lovely waterfalls at Cam Spout. The stream later runs out on to the broad and boggy floor of Great Moss, where few walkers venture to tread. Watch for a path bearing right, hugging the fellside to stay clear of Great Moss, and passing beneath scree below Cam Spout Crag.

When the path runs closer to the infant River Esk as it leaves Great Moss, look out for a point where the river can be crossed easily, and continue downstream using a path on the opposite bank. After turning a boggy corner, the River Esk drops more steeply at Esk Falls, and the delightful Lingcove Bridge later throws its stone span across Lingcove Beck, a river blessed with fine waterfalls worthy of exploration.

Follow the wide, obvious path downstream after crossing Lingcove Bridge. This path runs close to Brotherilkeld Farm, where the farm access road leads to the road at the foot of Hardknott Pass. Turn right and follow the road across Whahouse Bridge to return to Wha House Farm.

20 Hard Knott

Hardknott Pass is well known both to motorists and walkers, but the fell of Hard Knott, from which it takes its name, is not so well known. This rugged little fell provides a short, but quite interesting walk. The most obvious attraction on its flanks is Hardknott Roman Fort – situated in a most unlikely position but with a commanding view along Eskdale. The ascent of Hard Knott from the fort is soon accomplished, and the walk can be extended along its hummocky crest, ending with a delightful series of waterfalls in Lingcove Beck.

Distance: 6 miles/10km
Height gain: 1,640ft/500m
Walking time: 4 hours
Type of walk: A

moderate fellwalk over rocky and boggy ground with some vague paths.
Start/Finish: Hardknott Roman Fort. GR219014.

There is only limited parking near Hardknott Roman Fort, halfway up the steep and twisting road crossing Hardknott Pass on the Eskdale side. A clear track runs a short way up from the road, and the ruins of Hardknott Fort are initially hidden. This walk is relatively short, so there should be plenty of time to explore the layout of the fort thoroughly. The square fort has rounded corners and it has been partially restored. A course of thin Lakeland slate marks the original height of the walls before restoration, on top of which collapsed masonry was added until there was no more left to build with.

There are four gateways – one in each of the four walls –
and the provision of a gateway on the north-western side
is odd, as anyone leaving that way in a hurry would fall
down a rugged slope! No doubt the fort was built to a set
plan and the doorway was constructed regardless of the
terrain. The gateway on the north-eastern side features a
discernible track which leads to a square, levelled area
overlooked by an earthen mound. This was the original
parade ground, and officers would have conducted drills
from the top of the mound.

Having reached this point, the walk has in effect
already started and might as well continue. Simply
aim for the motor road and follow it to the top of
Hardknott Pass.

It's surprising how many cars cross over the top of
Hardknott Pass with their engines still racing in
low gear, as if not quite convinced that the climb is
over! For walkers, the climb is only just beginning,
and they need to engage low gear themselves.
There is a path leaving the highest part of the road
which outflanks nearby crags and rocky gullies
The climbing is over too soon and all that remains
is to wander along the broad and hummocky crest
of the fell looking for the highest point. There seem
to be many contenders, but there is a cairn on the
true summit at 1,803ft/552m.

Despite the modest altitude of the fell, the view is very
good. Higher fells are grouped all around, and the Scafell
range displayed in all its glory. The back side of Crinkle
Crags has little to commend it, while more distant view
take in the peak of Harter Fell and the Coniston Fells
There is also a fine view along the length of Eskdale.

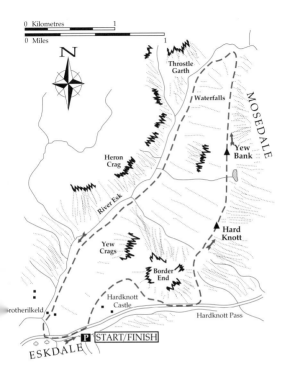

only a short walk is required, take great care to retrace
steps carefully to Hardknott Pass, as it is easy to become
stranded on some of the crags frowning over the road.

To continue with the walk, however, simply
continue onwards from the summit cairn,
following the hummocky, boggy crest of the fell
roughly northwards. In clear weather there are no
difficulties, but in mist it is easy to become
disorientated. In these conditions it would be

inadvisable to descend into Eskdale. The broad northern slopes run towards Lingcove Beck and once the river is reached all that is needed is a left turn to start following it downstream.

Lingcove Beck is fairly unremarkable at first, but later it descends with more vigour, and it is worth leaving the path to peer into the rocky gorge through which the river runs. There are some splendid waterfalls and deep, green plunge-pools, overhung by exotic ferns and hardy rowans. It is an enchanting, secret world, and many walkers on the nearby path are quite unaware of it. The lovely stone span of Lingcove Bridge is found at the confluence of Lingcove Beck and the River Esk.

Continue downstream alongside the Esk following a clear path roughly parallel to the river. This path passes close to Brotherilkeld Farm whose access road quickly leads to the road at the foot of the Hardknott Pass. There are notices flanking the road which warn of the sharp bends and severe gradients on one of the worst public roads in England. Walkers can follow the road, but might prefer a path branching left above a patch of woodland. This leads back to Hardknott Fort which can be explored a second time before leaving.

DUDDON VALLEY

The Duddon Valley must be one of the Lake District's least well known dales. It has no lake and no large settlements and few obvious features of interest. Those who take the trouble to explore it properly, however, will discover a charming and varied landscape full of interest. There are many fine walks which can be enjoyed in and around the Duddon Valley, and a selection of three are described in this section.

The Dunnerdale Fells are a tightly knit little group of fells in between the lower part of the Duddon Valley and the hamlet of Broughton Mills. They offer an interesting horseshoe circuit and are aggressively knobbly despite their modest stature. The walk starts and finishes at the Blacksmith's

Christine Isherwood

The Duddon at Birks Bridge

Arms. Caw is an amazing fell which appears as a prominent pyramid of rock in some views, rather like a mini-Matterhorn. A walk over Caw can be accomplished from the hamlet of Seathwaite, starting and finishing from the Newfield Inn, using a number of fine old roads which have been cut across the fells. Harter Fell is the fell which dominates the head of the Duddon Valley, and is a prominent sight for motorists engaged on the crossing of the Hardknott and Wrynose Passes. A route is offered on to Harter Fell using waymarked walks in Hardknott Forest.

The only public transport service in the Duddon Valley is a Post Bus, and walkers who use it must be careful to study its timetables. Whichever way motorists approach the Duddon Valley, they will have to follow narrow, winding roads featuring many steep gradients. The journey is worth the effort, as the dale is a marvellous place to walk and explore. There are only a handful of places to stay in the area, with food and drink being limited to a couple of pubs unless travelling out of the area. There is only a solitary post office shop in the dale with most commerce being directed through Broughton-in-Furness.

Sheep rearing and forestry are the two most noticeable activities in the Duddon Valley, though there are plenty of signs of former slate quarrying too. The place names throughout the dale are pure Norse and are a delight to the ears. The late poet Norman Nicholson, who lived nearby in Millom had a special affection for the Duddon Valley.

21 Dunnerdale Fells

Most fellwalkers have heard of Pike of Stickle in Great Langdale, but few have heard of Stickle Pike and Great Stickle. These little-known heights are part of the Dunnerdale Fells, a compact and rugged little range rising between Broughton and the Duddon Valley. A splendid circuit around these knobbly fells can be attempted from the hamlet of Broughton Mills, where the Blacksmith's Arms is located. This is one of the most traditional little hostelries in the Lake District, and again is hardly known to most visitors.

Distance:
5 miles/8km
Height gain:
1,640ft/500m
Walking time: *3 hours*
Type of walk:

Fellwalking, including some steep and rugged slopes with only vague paths.
Start/Finish: *Broughton Mills. GR223905.*

Parking is rather tight in Broughton Mills, but patrons of the Blacksmith's Arms might be able to negotiate for space in the pub car park.

Walk downhill through the hamlet of Broughton Mills and cross a bridge over the River Lickle. The road bends to the right, but aim straight onwards instead to follow the access road leading past Green Bank. This continues towards Scrithwaite Farm, but turn off to the left before reaching the buildings to follow an old lane. Look out for an old barn beside the lane a little later. A peep inside reveals that the building is supported by an enormous cruck-frame; there are very few Lakeland buildings still featuring this type of architecture.

Follow the lane only a little further, then bear to the right and start to pick a way up the steep slopes of Great Stickle. Rocky outcrops can be outflanked by following a vague path, and after a short ascent the summit trig point will be reached at 1,000ft/305m. There are already fine views around southern Lakeland, but the walker's attention is likely to be devoted to a careful study of the handful of little fells making up this circuit, as they are revealed as having quite steep and rugged slopes in places. To proceed beyond Great Stickle, it is a good idea to follow the broad and knobbly crest of the fell towards the peak of Stickle Pike. There are small pools couched in rocky, boggy hollows which lend an air of enchantment to the walk, and a path linking them has appeared.

A direct ascent of Stickle Pike looks steep, rocky and difficult, but by stepping to the right of the rocky peak an easier line to the summit will be spotted. There is a cairn at 1,231ft/276m and a fine prospect is revealed along the length of the Duddon Valley to Black Combe and the Duddon Estuary. The nearby summit of Caw looks particularly rugged and further towards the head of the Duddon Valley Harter Fell raises itself skywards, backed by even taller heights including the Scafell range. Retrace steps slightly to descend

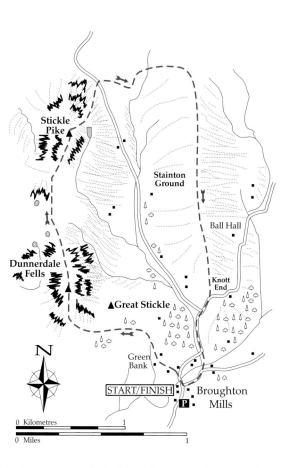

and keep to the left of Stickle Tarn to follow a clear path down to the highest point of a minor road. This road runs between Broughton Mills and the Duddon Valley, and is free of walls and fences as it crosses the high gap.

Cross straight over the road and walk towards the quarries above Stainton Ground. Watch where each footfall lands as there are some gaping holes in the ground where slate was formerly quarried. The courses of clear tracks proceed towards the old quarries. Climb up towards the quarries, but keep bearing to the right without entering them. After passing the last quarry, climb uphill to gain the hummocky crest of the fell above.

By walking roughly southwards along the crest of the fell, the rugged prow of Raven's Crag can be reached at its end. By keeping a little to the left on the descent from Raven's Crag it is possible to avoid the roughest part of the slopes which descend towards the next broad gap. There is a track which curves around the base of Raven's Crag; simply cross over it and climb on to the little hump of The Knott at 925ft/284m. This is the final summit on this circuit around the Dunnerdale Fells, so take a last look around at the view from this height.

There is another rugged patch of ground to be crossed on the descent from The Knott, then it is simply a case of walking down to the junction where the access road from the farm at Knott End joins a minor road. Turn right to follow the road downhill to a junction with another minor road. A left turn leads past a small chapel and crosses a bridge over the River Lickle to return to Broughton Mills and the Blacksmith's Arms.

22 Seathwaite and Caw

Caw is a small word to describe a rugged fell which in some views appears as a fine pyramidal peak. It is an outlier of the Coniston Fells and could equally be claimed by the Duddon Valley. The easiest approaches are from the Duddon Valley, although the fell itself has some steep, rugged and difficult slopes. Although an ascent of Caw could be combined with walks over neighbouring fells, it makes a fine objective in its own right, and the route offered here commences at the tiny hamlet of Seathwaite in the Duddon Valley.

Distance: 6 miles/10km	Fellwalking, with good paths, no paths, rocky and boggy ground.
Height gain: 1,540ft/470m	**Start/Finish:**
Walking time: 4 hours	Seathwaite, Duddon Valley. GR227960.
Type of walk:	

There are only limited parking places around the tiny hamlet of Seathwaite, so park considerately or ask for permission if in doubt. The only public transport service is a post bus, and if relying on this then be sure to check the timetables carefully.

Start on a road bend next to the Newfield Inn, where a gate gives access to a woodland at the very foot of Caw. The track bends to the right to enter the wood and is quite stony in places. Follow it uphill across the wooded slope and continue across the fellside beyond.

The track is known as Park Head Road and it runs parallel to a drystone wall throughout the ascent. There is a turning off to the left which serves Caw Quarry, but don't take it. Instead, continue along the track as if aiming for a gap in the fells ahead. Take the next path off to the left, climbing into a boggy little valley which is frowned upon by the rugged end of Caw known as Goat Crag. Choose any point at which to start climbing directly up the flanks of Caw, but keep well clear of Goat Crag. Pauses for breath may be required on this steep and rugged slope, but any difficulties are easily outflanked. The summit peak and trig point appear quite suddenly at 1,735ft/529m.

As Caw is such a prominent and steep-sided fell, views from it are good despite its modest height. There is a fine sense of depth in the prospect along the Duddon Valley, which is remarkably varied throughout its length. The northern panorama takes in Harter Fell at the head of the Duddon Valley and the lofty Scafell range. South-westwards, the whaleback form of Black Combe gives way to views of the coast, continuing around Morecambe Bay and embracing the Pennines more to the east. The Coniston Fells, although close at hand, are not seen to their best advantage.

A fairly gently graded descent can be accomplished by heading roughly eastwards from the summit. This avoids the rugged little hump of Pikes, but is nevertheless pathless and needs care in mist. It is

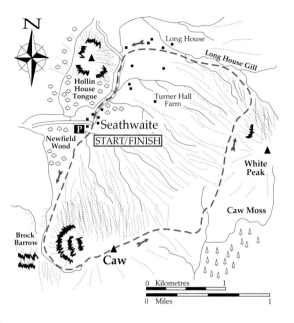

best to aim for the higher parts of a forestry plantation which sweeps down towards the River Lickle. There is a track rising up from the Lickle Valley and when this is reached, simply turn left and follow it uphill away from the forest. There are some very boggy patches at a higher level which may need to be outflanked, but firmer ground is gained on the slopes of White Pike.

The track being followed contours around the upper slopes of White Pike, and there is an opportunity to visit a couple of defunct quarries which are interesting. Continuing onwards across the slope, the course of the Walna Scar Road is joined, and this can be used to descend quickly and easily back into the Duddon Valley.

The route was once an important link between Coniston and the Duddon Valley, and has accommodated packhorse traffic, miners and quarrymen in its time. These days, almost all its travellers are walkers.

The Walna Scar Road runs parallel to Long House Gill as it descends from the fells, and it continues as a narrow tarmac road into the lower parts of the dale. When a junction is reached with another minor road, turn left to return to Seathwaite. It is worth making little diversions off this road to have a look at Tarn Beck alongside.

After heavy rain it displays some powerful waterfalls. Many casual visitors have mistaken it for the River Duddon, which pursues a parallel course some distance away in the awesomely rocky Wallowbarrow Gorge.

Walkers with time to spare might like to walk the short distance from Seathwaite to the Wallowbarrow Gorge, where a fine packhorse bridge spans the River Duddon in a graceful arch.

If no detours are to be made then a little chapel is passed just before the road reaches the Newfield Inn.

23 Harter Fell

Harter Fell has one foot in Eskdale and one foot in the Duddon Valley. As it is separated from neighbouring fells by the gap of Hardknott Pass, it is usually climbed purely for its own sake. The Eskdale flanks are rugged open fellside, while the slopes rising from the Duddon Valley are swathed in the conifers of Hardknott Forest. A combination of waymarked forest trails and open fellside make a varied circuit from the Duddon Valley, starting and finishing at the beauty spot of Birks Bridge.

Distance:
6 miles/10km
Height gain:
1,500ft/460m
Walking time: 4 hours
Type of walk: Forest
paths and tracks giving
way to fellwalking where
paths may be vague.
Start/Finish: Near Birks
Bridge, Duddon Valley.
GR235995.

Cars can be parked at a riverside car park a little way upstream from Birks Bridge, which spans the River Duddon as it flows through an attractive rocky gorge. There is a Post Bus service running through the Duddon Valley, and if walkers are relying on it they should check the timetables carefully.

Walk back down the road a short way from the car park to Birks Bridge. There are notices explaining about the range of colour-coded forest trails available.

Pause for a while on Birks Bridge to admire the rocky gorge, then try and obtain a view of how gracefully the bridge spans the gorge. A woodland track leads quickly uphill to Birks. This was formerly a farm, but now serves as a field centre, and it remains standing in a clearing while the land around it has been forested. Continue uphill a short way, then turn left to follow a wide forest track. The track climbs gradually uphill in a series of loops, and it is necessary to keep right at a junction further ahead. The left-hand track leads off-route towards Grassguards. The track peters out in an area which has been clear-felled, although there is a path leading onwards to the edge of the forest.

When the forest fence is reached and open fell lies beyond, turn right to start walking uphill. The forest runs only a short way up this slope, so that walkers are quickly left on the open fell. The path is fairly clear and the slope is quite steep, but there are no real difficulties on the ascent. A wider trodden path rising from Eskdale is soon joined and this leads onwards to the summit. Walkers who were initially disappointed that only a single fell was to be climbed may be heartened to find that it boasts three distinct summits. There is a trig point sitting on top of one boss of rock at 2,140ft/653m, but there are two other upthrusts of rock which rise even higher. Both alternative summits can be reached by short, rocky scrambles.

The Scafell and Coniston Fells feature well in the view, and there are more distant prospects towards the fells around Wasdale, as well as to Fairfield and High Street.

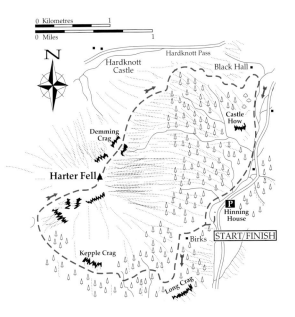

To the south and west are stretches of coastline, as well as the long ridge of moorland which terminates with the distant hump of Black Combe. In very clear weather the Isle of Man will be spotted. Also remarkable, owing to the shape of the landscape, is a plan view of Hardknott Roman Fort on the Eskdale side of Hardknott Pass.

The descent from the summit of Harter Fell leads towards Hardknott Pass. The best line is to start dropping downhill steeply to the north-east, as if aiming for the forest fence. Don't go all the way to the fence, but aim to stay on the open fell. The important thing is to avoid Demming Crag, which is a significant obstacle. There is a vague path, which needs to be followed carefully across a rugged fellside composed of hummocks and boggy patches.

There is no need to go all the way to the road on Hardknott Pass, but turn right around the far corner of the forest. A direct descent could be made alongside the forest to land on lower ground, but look out for signs of an old track which zigzags down the boggy slope. This old track is a remnant of the Roman road which once crossed Hardknott Pass.

Turn left towards the bottom of the slope to try and trace the old road through fields towards Black Hall, the isolated farm seen ahead. Turn sharply right on the final approach to the farm and walk across the fields to reach the banks of the River Duddon. Follow the river downstream and it leads back towards the forest. Note the splendidly rocky excrescence of Castle How, on the slopes above, which does look rather like a ruined castle. There is a strip of land bearing a path between the forest and the river, and this leads to a bridge which returns walkers to the car park where the circuit began.

CONISTON

Signs of industry and commerce abound around Coniston, which has grown from a little village into something approaching a small town. The Coniston Fells and more especially Coniston Old Man loom large over the village, while lower hills spread away to the south and east. The village has a full range of facilities, including shops and abundant accommodation of all types. There are outdoor gear retailers and two Youth Hostels. The place is a magnet for fellwalkers and there is a good range of bus services.

Three very varied walks are described in this section. To the south of Coniston, the rugged Beacon Fells offer a short walk encompassing Coniston Water, Beacon Fell and Beacon Tarn. A network of paths thread through this area, which would otherwise be very rough underfoot. The Coniston Fells offer all sorts of possibilities for walks, as there are so many summits, ridges, paths

Chris East

Coniston

and ways to link them all together.

The walk described around the Coniston Fells is a fairly basic circuit, but one which allows for all sorts of variations if the weather is fine and the walker is full of energy. Views from the tops in clear weather can be remarkably wide ranging.

The third walk starts at the popular beauty spot of Tarn Hows. Although most people stroll only around the tarn, this walk is taken around Holme Fell to explore neighbouring Tilberthwaite to offer a longer and more varied outing. Despite extensive quarrying in the area, and much more interference by man, the circuit is most charming and entertaining.

The Ruskin Museum in Coniston is not exclusively dedicated to John Ruskin, but also includes exhibits about the life and industry of the area. There is a collection of minerals and a number of items relating to Donald Campbell's disastrous water speed attempt on Coniston Water. Students of industrial archaeology could stay amid a scene of despoilation in the Coppermines Youth Hostel and roam around the Coppermines Valley exploring shafts, adits, levels, spoil heaps and old tramways. Apart from the copper mines, there is considerable scarring by slate quarrying, although nature is beginning to soften many of these sites with greenery.

24 Beacon Fell

Blawith is a scattered little village and although it looks fairly prosperous an old verse tells how the inhabitants had to struggle to buy themselves a church bell. "As poor as hell / They had to sell / A bit of fell / To buy a bell." Although the Blawith Fells are of modest height and of limited extent, they are also quite rugged and feature plenty of thorny scrub, rocky outcrops, boggy patches - as well as being notable for their population of adders! The ascent of Beacon Fell and the circuit of Beacon Tarn is worth the effort involved.

Distance: 5 miles/8km
Height gain: 690ft/210m
Walking time: 3 hours
Type of walk: Simple fellwalking, mostly on good paths, with some rocky and boggy patches.
Start/Finish: Brown Howe Car Park, Coniston Water. GR291912.

The Brown Howe Car Park is situated in a wooded area on the shores of Coniston Water between Blawith and Oxen Park. It is a charming little place when quiet, having a short stretch of lakeshore access. There are also picnic tables and a toilet block on site.

Leave the car park and turn left along the main road, then almost immediately turn right along a dead-end minor road. This leads into the Blawith Common Access Area, which is quickly revealed as an area of scrubby woodlands, rocky outcrops and boggy areas graced with plants such as bog myrtle. Juniper bushes might also be noticed at the start of this walk.

Anyone worried about encountering adders can be assured that adders have no wish to encounter people, and generally slip away unnoticed long before they are seen. If an adder is spotted, count it as an extra attraction, but do not approach or attempt to touch it. Adder bites are seldom dangerous, but the discomfort endured after receiving one is best avoided by leaving the poor creature alone in the first place!

Follow the narrow road uphill. It leads towards the farm of Stable Harvey, but shouldn't be followed all that way. There is a drystone wall on the right-hand side of the road and later a rough and knobbly ridge rises on the left-hand side. Leave the road and aim to follow this rugged ridge uphill, linking together a series of vague paths as height is gained. The ridge is nowhere near as rugged as it looks, but walkers will appreciate that some routes in this area must be desperately difficult, so it is advisable to keep to the paths.

The summit cairn on Beacon Fell is reached fairly quickly and it stands at an altitude of 836ft/255m. It is the highest of a handful of rugged summits in the Blawith Fells.

Views northwards take in the higher Coniston Fells, which effectively block a view of many more Lakeland fells, but the Helvellyn and High Street ranges can be seen, as well as Black Combe, stretches of coastline

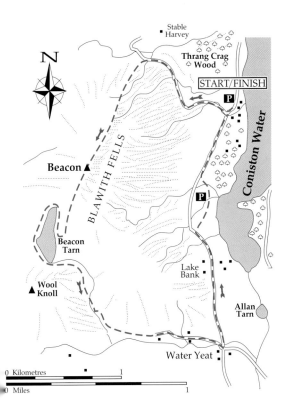

around Morecambe Bay and the distant Pennines. The
eye is drawn to the sight of Beacon Tarn couched in its
moorland hollow at the foot of Beacon Fell, and this is the
next objective on the walk.

There is a clear path running down from the
summit cairn on Beacon Fell to reach the stream
flowing out of Beacon Tarn. However, walkers will

also notice that there is a path encircling the tarn, and this is a recommended inclusion in the route. The path is narrow in places, and there are a couple of muddy stretches, but the tarn is charming and it is as well to make the most of it. This little circuit needs to end back at the outflowing stream.

A clear path accompanies the stream flowing down from Beacon Tarn towards Water Yeat. The path quickly becomes a stony track and then a tarmac road before reaching the charming little hamlet of Water Yeat. Turn left to walk away from Water Yeat along the main road for a while. The road is fenced in such a way that it has the appearance of a parkland drive, but in the summer months it can be busy with traffic and this effect is lost. After passing Lake Bank the road is unfenced for a while and a notice again announces that the land is part of a designated Access Area.

To make the most of this little stretch of open country, turn to the right and leave the main road. Walk across the rugged common to reach the shore of Coniston Water, but note that this path can be underwater when the lake level is high. It is almost immediately necessary to head back towards the main road, but the short break from the road will be deemed a pleasant interlude. Turn right along a wooded stretch of the main road to return quickly to the Brown Howe Car Park where the walk began.

25 Coniston Fells

There are dozens of ways to arrange walks around the Coniston Fells, as there are so many ways up and down, so many summits to include or exclude, and so many other points of interest such as mining, quarrying, rock-climbing, etc. The route offered here is a circuit taking in the main crest of the range, but also offering splendid views of Dow Crag, and hinting at the wealth of industrial heritage in the form of quarries and copper mines. With extra effort, the fells of Dow Crag, Grey Friar and Wetherlam could be added to the round.

Distance:
8 miles/13km
Height gain:
2,065ft/630m
Walking time: 6 hours
Type of walk: Classic

fellwalking, mostly on good paths, including steep and rugged slopes.
Start/Finish: *Walna Scar Road, above Coniston.* GR289971.

Motorists can get a bit of a leg-up to the start of this walk by driving up the narrow Walna Scar Road from the Sun Inn in Coniston. Anyone arriving by bus will have to walk up the road. Cars can be parked beyond the fell gate in a small quarry just after the tarmac expires. It is important to close the fell gate securely to prevent sheep wandering down into Coniston.

The Walna Scar Road continues as a rough surfaced track around the southern slopes of

137

Coniston Old Man. Walkers can get into their stride by following this clear track, preparing themselves for tougher fellwalking further along.

There is another track heading off steeply uphill to the right, but avoid this as it ends in a working slate quarry which is both dangerous and forbidden to walkers. The Walna Scar Road continues around the flanks of Coniston Old Man, and after wet weather one stretch can be deep underwater. Further along, the track narrows, becomes quite stony, and is sometimes confined to cuttings in the bedrock. As it climbs uphill, keep an eye peeled to spot a large heap of stones, where another path heads off to the right. If a bridge with railings is reached, then steps will have to be retraced slightly to search for the path.

The path climbs up alongside a broad and boggy valley, then climbs more steeply amid boulders and outcrops of rock. The immense, frowning face of Dow Crag assures walkers that they are on the right course, but timid walkers may find the prospect daunting. After climbing over a brow of rock the little tarn of Goat's Water is found couched in a wild hollow at the foot of Dow Crag's bouldery screes. It was on Dow Crag that pioneers of Lakeland rock-climbing practised, and names such as Haskett-Smith, Slingsby and Hopkinson are forever associated with these buttresses and gullies. The five big buttresses are known among rock-climbers as A, B, C, D & E. Routes such as Easy Gully and Easy Terrace are beyond the scope of many fellwalkers, who prefer to use their hands only in extremes!

Follow the path along the bouldery shore of Goat's Water, then climb out of the rocky dale-head using the path which is blazed up to the gap between Dow Crag and the Old Man. Parts of this path are quite badly worn, so walk with due care and consideration. It is as well to pause on the gap to regain breath and if the day is misty then it would also be sensible to make a careful study of the map before proceeding further. The Coniston Fells are covered by a network of paths and it is essential that walkers remain alert and never blithely assume that the path they are following is the path they should be following!

There is a path climbing eastwards from the top of the gap, and it gradually swings south-eastwards as it crosses the rather featureless back slopes of the Old Man. By keeping to the right there should be no problem joining the path which has been trodden along the main crest of the fell, ending suddenly at the huge platform cairn which crowns the summit. There is a trig point nearby, but the extra height of the platform cairn brings the top of Coniston Old Man to an altitude of 2,633ft/803m.

Views have a great sense of depth as the slopes fall away to Coniston and Coniston Water without other heights to challenge the Old Man. Morecambe Bay, the distant Pennines and North Wales could be featured. Only in the opposite direction are any notable Lakeland fells to be observed, and they are crowded around the skyline from west to north to east. Although the crest of the Coniston Fells tends to dominate, this changes later on in the walk.

Retrace steps for a short way along the crest of the

fell, being careful not to be drawn back down the path towards Dow Crag. The narrow ridge used on this descent offers fine views down onto the blue-green tarn of Low Water, then the crest of the fells broadens considerably as it climbs gently, so that Brim Fell appears more like a football pitch than a fell. A small heap of stones graces its summit at 2,611ft/795m. The path continues northwards, and the broad crest becomes a narrow ridge as it leads downhill. The next gap is Levers Hause, where walkers stand perched between Levers Water and Seathwaite Tarn.

The next steep climb uphill reaches a break of slope at the top of Great How Crags. In mist, it is important to recognise this fact. Some walkers assume that they are on Swirl How, and are then led to make a dangerous descent along what they assume is Prison Band. Keep an eye on the map and continue northwards along the broad ridge to reach the true summit of Swirl Fell, which is crowned by a large cairn at 2,630ft/802m. Views around the Lakeland Fells are considerably enhanced, and the view through to Langdale is particularly good. As from the Old Man earlier every notable range of fells is in view, but from this airy perch more of their flanks can be seen. More distantly, in clear weather, the view can embrace everything from the Isle of Man to the Pennines.

Descend eastwards from Swirl How's summit down the rocky ridge of Prison Band. Although this is steep and rugged for most of the descent, it also bears a clear path leading down on to a prominent gap, and provided that this path is used

here should be no difficulty. Once the gap is reached, turn right and follow a clear path down across the flanks of Black Sails. This path lands beside the shores of Levers Water. Continue to the outflowing stream, where there is an artificial dam, and cross to the far side. (Walkers who are aiming to catch a bus in Coniston might prefer to continue down through the Coppermines Valley in preference to the rest of the route described below.)

Climb uphill from the ouflow of Levers Water, passing a huge funnel of a hole which is one of several entrances to a honeycomb of underground copper mines. Tread warily on this particular patch of fellside, and do not go near any holes. Cross over a little gap in the fells, then follow a path down into an area known as Boulder Valley. The reason for this name will be obvious, and after crossing a wooden bridge over a stream the enormous Pudding Stone can be inspected.

Looking up towards Coniston Old Man, slate quarries and ruined inclines are stacked one on top of another practically to the summit of the fell. Looking down into the Coppermines Valley, the spoil heaps and ruins of the mining industry can be seen. The area is an absorbing study for anyone interested in industrial heritage.

Follow a clear path and track which contours out of Boulder Valley reaching a slaty track used as a line of ascent to Coniston Old Man. Turn left to walk down this only a short way, then turn right to follow another clear track over a little gap in between the Old Man and the rugged hump known as The Bell. This track leads straight across the lower slopes of the Old Man to return walkers to the car park by the fell gate on the Walna Scar Road.

26 Tarn Hows

One of the most popular places in Lakeland for taking a stroll is Tarn Hows. Reached by a minor road between Coniston and Hawkshead, Tarn Hows can be busy in the summer, and yet deserted in the winter. Many merely potter along the paths, while others are content to make a circuit of the tarn. With more time to spare it is worth extending the walk to embrace the flooded quarry at Hodge Close and the rocky gorge at Tilberthwaite.

Distance:
7¹/₄ miles/12km
Height gain:
1,000ft/305m
Walking time: 4 hours
Type of walk: Basically low level, well wooded, along clear paths, tracks and roads.
Start/Finish: Tarn Hows. GR326996.

Follow the one-way road system and park at a forest car park, then stand beside the road overlooking the area and spend a moment observing the scene. Tarn Hows is not a natural feature, but was formerly three small pools whose level was raised. There is a circular path around Tarn Hows, and it is as well to use the stretch round the eastern side to start the walk.

Walk onwards until the path turns noticeably round the northern end of the water, then look out for a path heading off to the right. This path wanders out of the woods and joins a clear gravel lane. Turn left to follow the lane, passing fields and woodlands before descending to the main A593 road beside Arnside Cottage. Turn right, then immediately left when crossing the main road, to start following the access road towards High Oxen Fell. There are good views before it begins to drop into woodlands around Hodge Close.

Just before joining the road at Hodge Close, there is an incline down to the left into an abandoned quarry. It is worth walking down into this quarry, which leads to a series of immense caverns cut from the slate. There is a metal gangway over a deep, cloudy pool which fills another abandoned quarry. Climbing back out of the quarry by the incline used to enter it, turn left to follow the road away from Hodge Close.

Follow the narrow, twisting road away from the quarries, passing through woodlands which serve to obscure views of other quarries. A group of buildings which are passed were once used to house quarrymen. Look out for a sign indicating a footpath through the woods on the right. The path simply wanders across the floor of the valley to link minor roads on either side of the valley. When the farm of High Tilberthwaite is reached, turn left to follow the road as far as a prominent rocky gorge.

The gorge at Tilberthwaite is an interesting distraction and walkers can make whatever explorations they wish, bearing in mind that they will have to return to the road. At the very least, it is worth penetrating the gorge to stand on one of the footbridges in its throat, from where

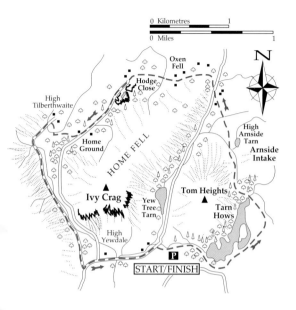

fine waterfalls can be seen. There are paths which rise on the slopes on both sides of the gorge, and the river is easily crossed at a higher level allowing both paths to be linked into a circuit. Return to the road and follow it through the valley to link with the main A593 road.

Turn left along the main road, passing the farmhouse of High Yewdale as the road runs past a number of fields. The road bends to the left at Glen Mary, where there is a car park on the right. Follow the path which climbs up through the woods alongside a stream, as this is the stream issuing from Tarn Hows, and the path leads straight up to the dam. From that point, simply walk back to the forest car park used at the start.

GRIZEDALE

Several areas of the Lake District are under forest cover, but the plantations at Grizedale are the most extensive. Formerly, this area was composed of open moorlands, fields and farms. The only fields and farms remaining are in the dale bottoms and in occasional breaks in the forest cover. The plantations date from the 1930s, so some stands have matured and have already been clear-felled. On the higher parts, the moorland cover quickly re-establishes itself, but as the newly planted trees grow higher, they will cut out the light and make the forest floor once again a sterile place.

There was a time when walkers venturing into Grizedale Forest did so without the benefit of waymarks and signposts, often using maps which didn't show all the forest tracks and paths. Bewildered and sometimes benighted, these walkers were not likely to encourage others to follow in their footsteps. It was often the practice for rangers to enter the forest in the evening and flush out any lost souls! Things have changed considerably and there are now several waymarked routes and helpful signposts. Maps now show a much clearer picture of the forest paths and tracks, and these are usually kept clear for walkers to follow.

Two walks are offered in this area. One starts and finishes at Grizedale, following a waymarked route known as the Silurian Way. There are also several curious sculptures tucked away in the forest, which have been erected by a number of artists. Before setting out be sure to pop into the Visitor Centre at Grizedale and pick up some of the forest maps and literature which help to make explorations more enjoyable. The other walk takes in Claife Heights, and is not nearly as forested as the walk from Grizedale. The route includes a stretch of the Windermere shore, woodlands, farms and fields, with an opportunity to visit Beatrix Potter's house at Hill Top.

Facilities on the walk from Grizedale are limited to those provided around the village. The Forestry Commission have provided a restaurant, along with a theatre, visitor centre and accommodation, including a campsite. On the walk around Claife Heights, there are places to eat and drink at Far Sawrey, while a ferry ride across Windermere brings the abundant facilities of Bowness within easy reach. Public transport includes the ferry across Windermere and a Post Bus service to Grizedale. Nearby Hawkshead has a more regular bus service linking with Coniston and Ambleside.

27 Silurian Way

There was a time when people used to venture deep into Grizedale Forest, got lost, and had to be flushed out by forest rangers in the evening. These days, a helpful series of colour-coded waymarked trails is available to visitors. Many take only an hour or two to complete, but the Silurian Way offers a longer circuit, running from Grizedale to Force Mills and back. Apart from forest tracks and paths to explore, there are several intriguing forest sculptures springing up in unlikely places, adding more interest to the walk.

Distance:
9¹/₄ miles/15km
Height gain:
1,640ft/500m
Walking time: 5 hours
Type of walk: A

*waymarked forest walk
using clear paths, tracks
and roads.*
Start/Finish: Grizedale
Forest Visitor Centre.
GR335944.

Parking is available at the Grizedale Forest Visitor Centre, which incorporates an information centre and restaurant – as well as the celebrated Theatre in the Forest. The "Ancient Forester" guards the car park and wields a huge axe, but there are plenty of other sculptures to be discovered, and it would be a pity to pass close to a good one without realising. They are continually developed and some of the earliest date from 1977.

Cross over the road outside the Visitor Centre, where a board marking the start of the Silurian Way has been fixed to a wall. Detailed directions are hardly necessary as the entire route is adequately waymarked using stout green-band posts. Look out for them at junctions of paths and tracks, and start getting suspicious if they haven't been seen for a while! An old track is used to gain height in the forest and there are odd sculptures to be noted alongside. A brochure explains that their "vitality springs from the sculptor's response to the forest and the questions it poses for their sculptural practice."

The broad forest tracks used at the start of this circuit climb uphill and swing to the right to run quite close to the lonely pool of Grizedale Tarn, although this will hardly be noticed without a short detour. The Silurian Way passes southwards through New South Wales Plantation where stands of mature trees contrast with clear-felled and replanted areas. As the forested slopes descend southwards, the route is brought down on to minor roads near Force Mills, where a right turn leads past Satterthwaite School in a lovely woodland glade. As an open area of fields is passed, watch out for a left turn where a track leads back into woodlands which later give way to forestry plantations.

Sculptures again abound, and it is worth looking out for "The Meeting" where three wooden figures are found in a conspiratorial huddle. On approaching you almost expect them to run for cover, taking their secrets with them!

The waymarked course of the Silurian Way uses forest tracks and paths which lead northwards after crossing Farra Grain Gill, gradually climbing towards the summit of Carron Crag, where a large area has been fenced off against deer. There is a trig point on top of this clear-felled rise at 1,030ft/314m.

As the trees have been cut back, and the new trees haven't gained any great height, views are surprisingly extensive. The Coniston and Langdale Fells are seen to good advantage, and the Helvellyn, Fairfield and High Street ranges are also displayed. The Pennines stretch away in the distance and far to the south is Morecambe Bay.

Descending from Carron Crag, the Silurian Way continues northwards before making several right turns to progress back towards the Visitor Centre. Walkers who are pressed for time could link with other waymarked trails which allow a more rapid descent. As there are a number of forest scupltures positioned all the way down the slopes, it is worth spending a little extra time searching for some of the more unusual specimens.

If there is still time to spare after returning to the Visitor Centre, then stroll along the short Ridding Wood Walk, which has plenty more strange sculptures, including an enormous wooden xylophone from which to beat a merry tune!

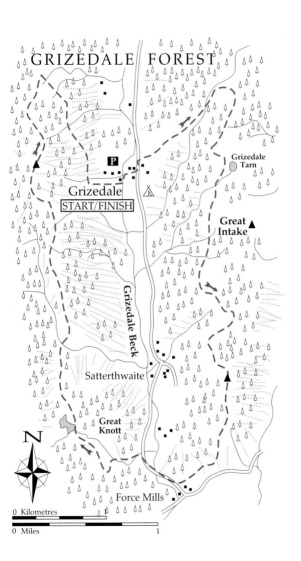

GRIZEDALE FOREST

Grizedale
START/FINISH

P

Grizedale
Tarn

Great
Intake

Grizedale Beck

Satterthwaite

Great
Knott

N

Force Mills

0 Kilometres

0 Miles   1

28 Claife Heights

It is known that when Wordsworth was schooled at Hawkshead he sometimes had to shout across Windermere to attract the attention of the ferryman. But who was the mysterious Crier of Claife whose ghostly wailing was sometimes heard at night across the lake? In daytime, there is nothing to fear and the scene is quite enchanting as the walk progresses along the lake shore, through woods and forests, taking in quaint little cottages and enjoying views towards the higher fells.

Distance: 7 miles/11km	woodland and field walk using good paths, tracks and roads.
Height gain: 590ft/180m	**Start/Finish:** Ferry House on the shore of Windermere. GR391956.
Walking time: 4 hours	
Type of walk: Low-level	

There are parking places just off the road which serves Ferry House, so do not park alongside the road where a car might obstruct traffic needing to use the ferry. Walkers can easily access this route from Bowness-on-Windermere by taking the short ferry ride across the lake to reach Ferry House. This costs only a few pence and the ferry runs from early until late each day.

To begin the walk, follow the road away from Ferry House, as if going to Far Sawrey. The road turns around a couple of points as it hugs the lake shore, then begins to climb uphill. There is a path available running parallel to the road, and this can be used to avoid competition from traffic while climbing up to a road junction.

Turn left and left again at a couple of junctions with minor roads, to start following the Lakeside road roughly parallel to the shore of Windermere. The road is at some distance from the lake and as there are often woods alongside it is not always possible to see the water. Stay on the road only until the large house called Fellborough has been passed. A footpath sign on the left indicates a route to the lake shore, but bear in mind that this path could be underwater when the lake level is high.

The path follows the shoreline and crosses a wooden footbridge over Cunsey Beck, before wandering around a wooded point. The rocky islet of Ling Holme is just offshore. The next rocky point is Rawlinson Nab, which is also wooded and completely encircled by the shore path. Follow the lakeshore onwards and the path will finally be diverted on to a minor road when the buildings of Holme Well are reached. Turn right to follow the road to the farm buildings at Low Cunsey.

A bridleway sign at Low Cunsey indicates a track on the left. Follow this track to a junction, then turn left again to continue along a narrower track. This passes the whitewashed ruins of The Forge. There may be some muddy patches to negotiate before the path reaches the next minor road. Turn right to follow the road only to the next junction at Eel House, then turn right again. A narrower road runs across Cunsey Beck, while further along the road a signpost indicates a path leading into Bishop Woods.

Follow the woodland path uphill and across a broad rise. The path leaves the woods and descends gently through fields to reach another minor road. Turn left to walk into the village of Far Sawrey. There is also an optional detour here, allowing the walker to follow a path on the left to reach Near Sawrey where Beatrix Potter's house – Hill Top – is located.

Apart from creating lovable animal characters in her series of children's books, Beatrix Potter was also deeply involved in conservation and left flocks of Herdwick sheep and a number of farms to the early National Trust. Hill Top can be an exceptionally busy place to visit, and there may be a lengthy queue. If it is included in the walk, then return to Far Sawrey afterwards to continue with the walk.

Turn right in Far Sawrey to pass a pub, then turn sharply left at a sign for Claife Heights. A clear track runs uphill above the pub and later bends to the right. Follow this track through a junction with another track, then pass to the left-hand side of a stand of trees. At the next signpost, turn right as indicated for the ferry.

A path runs along the wooded brow of Claife Heights, offering occasional views across the waters of Windermere before it descends through the woods to reach the roadside. Simply turn left to follow the road back towards Ferry House, or to

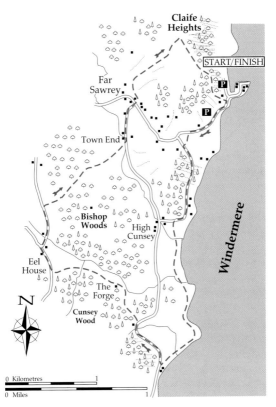

whichever car park was used at the start of the walk. Anyone returning by ferry as a foot passenger to Bowness-on-Windermere will have only a few minutes to wait for the next crossing.

LANGDALE

Langdale is the "long valley" of the Norse, stretching from the head of Windermere to the foot of Bow Fell. At the Windermere end it is fairly broad and flanked by low wooded hills and rugged little Loughrigg Fell. As the visitor progresses up the dale the distinctive outline of the Langdale Pikes dominates the scene. Langdale splits at its head into the rugged recesses of Oxendale and Mickleden, from which the only escape is to follow steep paths winding up rugged fellsides.

There are three walks described in Langdale, and all feature a network of paths which offers scope for variations. Starting from the lovely village of Elterwater, there is an ascent of the hummocky Loughrigg Fell. Despite its small stature, the fell is like a whole range of fells, threaded by paths and featuring a multitude of minor summits.

At the head of Langdale, lordly Bow Fell and the many summits of Crinkle Crags form an entertaining circuit around the top of Oxendale.

Christine Isherwood

Blea Tarn and the Langdale Pikes

This rugged walk can be confusing in mist, when care needs to be taken from summit to summit.

The third walk is a classic tour of the Langdale Pikes. This route can be varied by scramblers prepared to grapple with the steep, rocky ascent of Jack's Rake, but an easier ascent is suggested around the back of Pavey Ark. The round includes Harrison Stickle, Pike o'Stickle and Loft Crag, with a descent by way of Dungeon Ghyll.

There are plenty of places to stay along the length of Great Langdale, from splendid hotels to B&Bs, hostels and campsites. There are also plenty of pubs offering food and drink. They all seem to be adept at catering for walkers, and the Old Dungeon Ghyll Hotel, known as the ODG, is the most traditional in appearance. There is a regular bus service from Ambleside to the ODG. Car parking at peak seasons can be difficult and cars which parked indiscriminately alongside the road cause a nuisance. At peak periods motorists might consider patronising the bus service for a change.

There has been a great deal of path reconstruction on all the routes described in this section, and it is important that walkers stick faithfully to the new routes which have been created. Do not short-cut zigzags or follow old eroded paths, as this causes unsightly scars to develop. Stay on the reconstructed paths and do not walk along the reseeded edges. Some walkers complain that the new paths are hard underfoot, but if they would only take their time they would find them quite acceptable.

29 Loughrigg Fell

Loughrigg is of modest stature, and yet proves to be a sprawling and incredibly hummocky fell. It is almost like a range of fells in miniature, and boasts an impressive network of paths woven like green ribbons across the rugged slopes. Many walkers would find Loughrigg a confusing place in mist, with all its humps, bumps, paths and tracks; but even if anyone were to lose their way, the paths and tracks would eventually lead down to safety. It would, however, be galling to reach safety on completely the wrong side of the fell!

Distance: 5 miles/8km	fellwalking with some steep slopes and care needed in mist.
Height gain: 1,080ft/330m	**Start/Finish:** Elterwater, Great Langdale.
Walking time: 3 hours	GR327047.
Type of walk: Moderate	

Loughrigg could be climbed from a number of places, such as Ambleside, Rydal, Grasmere, Brathay and Skelwith Bridge, but this route starts and finishes in Elterwater.

Two roads lead quickly towards the open slopes of Elterwater Common, which is crossed by a number of paths. Use any path to ascend to the minor road seen cutting across the higher slopes of the common.

By turning right, this road could be followed through a gap at High Close, but to cut out a stretch of road walking it is better to follow a fell path through the slightly higher gap a short way to the west. The whole fellside is riddled with paths, so choose between the ones which funnel themselves through the rugged gap. Once the gap is being crossed, however, it is necessary to start choosing paths more carefully. Keep to the right-hand side of the gap, following a path running between two walled woodlands to reach a minor road on Red Bank. Just across the road a track flanked by walls and trees runs downhill on to Loughrigg Terrace.

While it is tempting to follow the broad and gently graded Loughrigg Terrace across the flanks of the fell, the object is to climb to the summit. Turn right to follow a steep path uphill. This has been reconstructed throughout its length, and provides a firm footing nearly all the way to the top of Loughrigg. The summit cairn and trig point stand at 1,099ft/335m – higher than all the other humps and bumps which are arranged along the sprawling crest of the fell.

Views from the top of Loughrigg are surprisingly extensive for a fell which is hemmed in by other heights two and three times its stature. There is a view roughly southwards along the length of Windermere, as well as northwards to the Skiddaw Fells. The Coniston Fells, Langdale Fells and Fairfield Horseshoe are all well displayed and there is a great feeling of depth to the view when the eye is drawn to the number of lakes in the lower parts of the dales.

In mist, the descent requires careful study of a map, and the use of a compass. It is difficult to say what does or does not constitute a path on Loughrigg. It is pointless to give "turn right, turn left" directions when so many paths criss-cross on these slopes. Worse than that, some paths split and rejoin! In clear weather, the rugged crest of the fell provides an entertaining romp, and walkers should head roughly south-eastwards towards the subsidiary summit of Ivy Crag. There is a fairly clear path going most of the way, but a detour from it will be needed to reach the top of the crag. There is a splendid view from Ivy Crag along the River Brathay and beyond towards the length of Great Langdale.

Looking straight down from Ivy Crag, a clear path will be spotted encircling the foot of the crag. Don't go straight down to it, as the way is too rocky, but retrace steps a short way and use other paths running downhill to reach it. By following this path down to Tarn Foot, near Loughrigg Tarn, a minor road can be joined and route finding becomes much easier. The path is quite stony on the descent, and when the road is joined it is necessary to turn right, then left to continue downhill towards Skelwith Bridge.

There is a pub by a road junction, and an ornamental slate works alongside. These can both be visited before continuing the walk. Leaving the slate works, follow a clear path which is sandwiched tightly between the B5343 road and the River Brathay. The river runs through a rocky gorge, and within a short time the powerfu

plunge of Skelwith Force will be seen and heard. After prolonged rain this is well worth admiring. There is a drawback, as prolonged rain also has the effect of submerging the path further onwards. A decision would need to be made in such conditions either to risk wet feet, or follow the road back to Elterwater.

The path generally stays close to the River Brathay, but does move away from it through some fields. There is a stretch of path alongside Elter Water too, but the lake is mostly screened from view by trees. Simply follow the clearest path onwards (or not, if it is underwater) towards Elterwater village and the car park.

30 Bow Fell and Crinkle Crags

Most fellwalkers would agree that Bow Fell is a fine enough objective in its own right, but combined with neighbouring Crinkle Crags a splendid day's walk becomes available around the rugged upper reaches of Langdale. Most walkers grind their way up the stony path on The Band to ascend Bow Fell by way of Three Tarns, but a much more interesting approach takes in the Climber's Traverse and the Great Slab. The rocky theme can be extended all the way along the immense switchback ridge of Crinkle Crags.

Distance:
8 miles/13km
Height gain:
3,280ft/1,000m
Walking time: 6 hours
Type of walk: Tough

fellwalking with plenty of steep rocky slopes needing care in mist.
Start/Finish: Old Dungeon Ghyll Hotel. GR285061.

The Old Dungeon Ghyll Hotel is the terminus for the bus service in Great Langdale, beside which is a National Trust car park. Backtrack a few paces to the road, then follow the access road across the level pastures to reach Stool End Farm, the last habitation in Great Langdale. A path rises steeply uphill from the farmyard, climbing up the rugged ridge known as The Band. It is a fine route and as height is gained there are widening views along the length of the dale and around the fells.

The initial steep slopes of The Band gradually ease and there is one stretch where the walking is almost level. Keep an eye peeled at this point to spot the Climber's Traverse heading off to the right, while the main path continues up towards Three Tarns. The Climber's Traverse is an entertaining route which cuts beneath a series of awesome crags and buttresses on the dark, almost sunless side of Bow Fell. Follow the path to the foot of Cambridge Crag, where water pours from the base of the cliff. Double back sharply to the left to climb up a steep and rugged slope, and the flat rocky slope of the Great Slab will be just alongside throughout the ascent. This is a remarkable feature, which later gives way to the rugged upper slopes of Bow Fell.

There is a path leading to the right across the top of Bow Fell, and this quickly leads on to a boulderfield. Pick a way gingerly across massive blocks and slabs to reach the summit of Bow Fell at 2,960ft/902m. There is no doubt at all that this is the summit, as the rocks are piled up almost into a sharp peak. It is a place to sit for a while, as the ascent has been steep and rugged almost all the way. Views are remarkably extensive. The immediate Langdale Fells and only slightly more distant Scafell range dominate by reason of their ruggedness.

Much was made in the past of the danger of taking a compass bearing on Bow Fell, citing magnetic rocks as upsetting readings. But there is no evidence to suggest that a compass properly used and held away from the body around chest level will be in any way affected. Any rocks containing magnetite or similar minerals would only be able to deflect a compass needle which was held quite close to them. In other words, trust the compass in mist and don't take chances by guessing the way off Bow Fell.

The only practicable course for walkers wanting to reach Crinkle Crags is to retrace steps slightly from the summit, then follow the path down a steep and stony slope to reach Three Tarns. These little pools sit on a hummocky gap and in very hot weather their number can be reduced as they are all quite shallow and dry up. Rising southwards beyond Three Tarns is the rugged, switchback ridge of Crinkle Crags. Walkers crossing these summits for the first time in poor visibility should pay particular attention to their maps, as it is possible to become disorientated. It would be disheartening for a party to grapple along this ridge for an hour only to land back at Three Tarns – but it does happen!

There are all sorts of rocky outcrops, pools of water and boggy bits along the crest of Crinkle Crags. The important feature to be aware of is that each successive "crinkle" rises a bit higher than the previous one. The ground rises in humps and bumps over Shelter Crags, then there are three distinct "crinkles" before the fourth one is revealed as the true summit at 2,816ft/860m.

In clear weather it is as well to pause and admire the view, as well as planning the next move, which could be

START/FINISH

Bow Fell

LANGDALE

The Old
Dungeon Ghyll Hotel

Three
Tarns

The Band

Stool End
Farm

Shelter
Crags

OXENDALE

Crinkle
Crags

Long Top

Great Knott

Pike of
Blisco

N

0 Kilometres 1

0 Miles 1

*tricky for more cautious walkers. In nasty weather, it
would probably be best to keep moving – and to avoid the
"Bad Step" which appears next.*

Walkers who stick to the clearest path leaving the
summit of Crinkle Crags are sometimes dismayed
to find themselves perched on the brink of a short
rock climb of some 10ft/3m leading down into a
gully. The gully would be a natural line to follow
were it not blocked by a huge wedged boulder, and
some walkers are quite prepared to squeeze
beneath this rather than attempt a climb down the
"Bad Step". There should be no problem if due care
is exercised, but if this obstacle is to be side-
stepped, then it is best to leave the summit of
Crinkle Crags using a lesser path further
westwards.

Either way, the path continues over one final
"crinkle" of no real consequence, then runs easily

down a long slope passing the minor summit of Great Knott to drop down towards Red Tarn. The sight of Pike of Blisco's fine form rearing up above the tarn might inspire some walkers to make an ascent, and this is to be commended, but other walkers will be ready to bring the walk to a close, and so the line of descent is given instead.

Cross the outflow from Red Tarn and turn left. A clear path begins to drop steeply downhill and it has been reconstructed in places. There are views to the left of the towering crags of the Crinkles, as well as Bow Fell and The Band, and it may surprise some walkers to take so long to cover what is really only a short distance. The path drops to the rugged floor of Oxendale, where Oxendale Beck has been channelled to control erosion and flooding. Cross over a bridge and follow the path down through the dale to return to Stool End Farm. The access road from the farm leads back towards the Old Dungeon Ghyll.

31 Langdale Pikes

The Langdale Pikes have a distinctive profile when seen from afar and as they are approached through Great Langdale they positively dominate the scene. They exude an air of impregnability, which is all the more surprising because they are riddled with paths. There is a classic circuit from pike-to-pike using paths which have become so worn they have had to be reconstructed. This is the basic route suggested below, but it is open to adaptation and can be extended in many ways by serious fellwalkers.

Distance: 5 miles/8km
Height gain: 2,300ft/700m
Walking time: 3 hours
Type of walk: Classic fellwalking with plenty of paths, but still needs care in mist.
Start/Finish: New Dungeon Ghyll Hotel, Great Langdale. GR294064.

There are a couple of car parks available near the New Dungeon Ghyll Hotel, where cautious walkers might already feel intimidated at the sight of the Langdale Pikes towering overhead. It all proves to be rather illusory, as there are some very clear paths scaling these heights and the summits can be gained from easier slopes at the back. It is important to note, before ascending via Mill Gill, that the path has been completely reconstructed in response to massive erosion. Some walkers still insist on following routes shown on out-of-date maps and guidebooks, creating further erosion on slopes which are only slowly regenerating. It is important to stick to the reconstructed paths, avoiding short-cuts, and certainly never climbing over barriers which have been erected to prevent the passage of walkers.

Start the walk behind the New Dungeon Ghyll Hotel and Stickle Barn complex, following the clear paths which have been constructed alongside Mill Gill. Some maps, guides and walkers call Mill Gill by the name of Stickle Ghyll – they are one and the same watercourse. Fine waterfalls can be observed on the ascent, and there is no difficulty with route finding as the stream issues forth from Stickle Tarn, which is revealed in due course. The sight of Pavey Ark's immense crag rearing up beyond Stickle Tarn is a good excuse for a pause.

Cautious walkers may be surprised to spot other walkers apparently grappling a way diagonally across the face of Pavey Ark. They are following the line of a difficult path known as Jack's Rake. This is a scramble which can be attempted by anyone with a head for heights who is prepared to use their hands, but it will not be followed on this walk.

Instead, keep to the path around the eastern side of Stickle Tarn and aim to go round the back of Pavey Ark before starting the ascent. The way is steep and rugged, but free of any real difficulty. The top of Pavey Ark is a hummocky patch of fell with no distinguishing characteristics at 2,288ft/697m. As it drops away so precipitously towards Stickle Tarn, explorations must be carried out with care, but there is certainly a fine view from the edge.

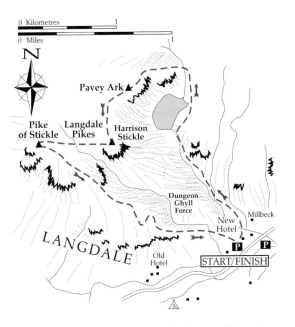

Clear weather is most helpful when walking from pike-to-pike, as this is a potentially confusing area of humps, bumps, rocky outcrops, patches of bog and paths which apparently wander aimlessly in all directions. The neighbouring summit of Harrison Stickle is roughly to the south-west, and is approached by keeping on a path which gradually curves towards it. Many maps show a direct line between the two summits, which is nonsensical. As Harrison Stickle is climbed from the high ground at its back, there is only minimal ascent. The summit is the highest of the Langdale Pikes at 2,403ft/732m.

This is a fine place to study the view along the length of Langdale, which has a great feeling of depth. Further afield all the other notable ranges of Lakeland Fells are in view, even though the dull moorland hump of High Raise tends to obscure the northern prospects.

There is a fairly direct path which heads from Harrison Stickle towards the striking, rocky dome of Pike of Stickle. There is a stream to cross in a boggy little valley, before the path begins to climb towards the dome. On the approach, walkers may wonder how to gain the summit. The standard ascent is a short rocky scramble from the far side. Once this is located, use it to reach the top, and bear in mind that it must also be used on the descent. The summit rises to 2,323ft/708m and is a grand place to stand. The rugged depths of Mickleden are literally underfoot, with rocky slopes soaring upwards to the summit of Bow Fell.

Worthy of note at this point is the Stone Axe Factory on South Scree which spills down from Pike of Stickle. A hard band of porcellanite running across the slopes of the fell has been worked in ages past to fashion stone axes. Numbers of "rejects" were cast on to the screes, but those which made the grade were sent out of the area for final polishing and some have been located even as far away as France! Archaeologists still look doubtfully at a cave cut from the porcellanite band beside the scree, but why else would it have been cut in such an unlikely place? South Scree has been devastated by people "running" the scree, and a visit is not recommended. In any case, foraging on the scree for "reject" axes is discouraged.

Carefully pick a way off the rocky dome by

retracing earlier steps, then consider the return route to the foot of the Pikes. On the way from Harrison Stickle to Pike of Stickle, the intervening hump of Loft Crag was probably scarcely noticed, but it is worth crossing before bringing the walk to a close. If the rugged crest is followed, then a path will be noticed towards its end, near Thorn Crag, dropping off to the right. This path is very clear and provides an excellent line of descent. After zigzagging on the upper slopes of the fells, it runs fairly close to the rocky cleft of Dungeon Ghyll. Hidden in the depths is a splendid waterfall, and a huge rock wedged to form a natural arch. This was a Victorian curiosity, and the early visitors gave the name "ghyll" to the ravine instead of the usual Lakeland "gill".

The path running alongside Dungeon Ghyll quickly deposits walkers back near the New Dungeon Ghyll Hotel, so that they can head for whichever car park was used at the outset. Few walkers leave without turning around and gazing one last time at the Langdale Pikes. They still look impregnable, even after each and every summit has been traversed.

GRASMERE

The lovely village of Grasmere occupies a splendid setting in the Vale of Grasmere, with a charming lake on one side and fine fells all around. The village is a natural launching point for a series of superb walks, with easy access to the fells and a full range of facilities for afterwards. This guidebook is part of a two volume series and the dividing line passes Grasmere as the Lake District is separated into East and West. Two walks are described to the west of the main road, while other walks can be found in the companion volume to this book.

One walk wanders up through Easedale, leaving the wooded lower parts of the dale and passing into the more rugged upper parts. The aim is to reach the crest of Blea Rigg, then follow the hummocky ridge back to Silver How before descending to Grasmere at the end of the walk. Keen walkers could extend this route to embrace Loughrigg Fell. The other walk is a horseshoe walk around the Greenburn Valley. It starts on Steel Fell, turns around the summit of Calf Crag and proceeds along Gibson Knott to reach Helm Crag. A final descent leads back into Grasmere.

Helm Crag's summit is one of the most peculiar Lakeland summits, with its rocky ridge featuring a number of interesting spikes of rock. These have gained nicknames over the years. The rocky sculptures on the crest of Helm Crag also present a difficulty for more cautious walkers, who may find the climb to the top of "The Howitzer" beyond their capabilities. There is a path which merely passes beside all the protruding rocks.

For its size, the village of Grasmere is packed with interest and facilities. Associations with William Wordsworth abound. The Wordsworth family plot is found at the parish church, while beyond the village is Dove Cottage and the Wordsworth Museum. There are plenty of gift shops and an unusual gingerbread shop, and many places offering food and drink. There are two Youth Hostels nearby, as well as B&Bs and hotels.

As a change from walking all the time, boats can be hired for a leisurely tour of the lake. Several buses pass backwards and forwards through Grasmere, linking with places such as Keswick, Ambleside, Windermere and Kendal. There are also a couple of large car parks and some smaller spaces. Even so, Grasmere can become very crowded at peak times and runs short of accommodation, parking spaces and other facilities.

Helm Crag

Donald Dakeyne

32 Blea Rigg

Between Grasmere and Great Langdale there is a long, knobbly ridge of fell bearing a number of rugged little summits. One of these is Blea Rigg, which can be ascended from Grasmere by walking along the length of Easedale. There are waterfalls and tarns to be enjoyed on this gradual ascent to the rugged crest. Both Blea Rigg and the lower summit of Silver How can be climbed on the way back to Grasmere, and in clear weather the humps, bumps and pools provide added interest.

Distance: 8 miles/13km	*fellwalking, with plenty*
Height gain:	*of paths, but care needed*
1,970ft/600m	*in mist.*
Walking time: 5 hours	**Start/Finish:** *Grasmere.*
Type of walk: Moderate	*GR 337076.*

Walk along Easedale Road. To avoid competition with traffic, walkers can use a path parallel to the road for a while, but the road must be followed again later. Look out for a slate-slab footbridge to the left of the road, then follow little signs for Easedale. A good track and path lead onwards towards the prominent waterfalls in Sour Milk Gill.

The path climbs uphill close to Sour Milk Gill, so that the milk-white cascade is seen to best effect. Above the waterfalls is Easedale Tarn, which is partly artificial as it has a dam constructed across

its outflow. As the path begins to climb uphill again, there are one or two quite steep and rocky stretches where the use of hands might be required. Looking off to the right, a splendid pyramidal peak of rock is noticed. This is Belles Knott, but it is largely an illusion as once the walker passes it and turns around, it appears only as a dull hump of grass. Keep following the path uphill until it joins a broader path on the crest of Blea Rigg.

Turn left to wander along the broad crest to locate the summit, which is a cairn on a rocky outcrop.

The summit area is not of any great significance, and the eye is more likely to be drawn towards the profile of the Langdale Pikes away to the west. The Pikes tend to obscure the distant prospect, so that other ranges in view include the Helvellyn, High Street and Coniston Fells. It should be noted that Blea Rigg has a confusing arrangement of knobbly tops, braided paths, pools of water and patches of bog. Walkers who are unfamiliar with it are advised to proceed cautiously in mist.

To start the long descent, walkers must attempt to follow the clearest path along the rugged crest of the fell. In very general terms this runs roughly south-eastwards, but there are so many twists and turns around minor summits, outcrops of rock and patches of bog that almost every point of the compass is featured. The path sometimes splits and rejoins, while at other times it may appear to do this but actually starts to lead down into Langdale or Grasmere at the wrong time. In clear weather there will be no problem and it is possible to enjoy lovely views along the way. There are a handful of rugged summits around Castle How, but the eye should be fixed on the more rounded hump of Silver How towards the end.

The grassy summit of Silver How bears a cairn at 1,292ft/394m. The view across the Vale of Grasmere is charming and the top of Blencathra can be seen peeping over the gap of Dunmail Raise. In other directions the Helvellyn, Fairfield and Coniston Fells are seen, as well as plenty of low country to the south. Take one last look back towards the Langdale Pikes, as these will quickly be lost to view on the final descent.

There are a couple of ways down from Silver How towards Grasmere, and both start on the northern side of the fell. Perhaps the scenery is a little better by dropping down a short, but steep little gully. Turn left along a path at the foot of this and follow a wall more gently downhill across the fellside. A gate in the wall gives access to a path running down to a minor road near the lake. Turn left to follow this road back into Grasmere, where every facility is available to satisfy a fellwalker.

33 Helm Crag

Generations of coach travellers have had the summit rocks of Helm Crag pointed out to them. Names for these curiously shaped protruberances include the Lion and the Lamb, the Lion Couchant, the Howitzer and the Old Woman Playing the Organ. They are intriguing from the roadside, and also prove worthy of a fellwalker's attention. This route makes a complete circuit high above the Greenburn Valley visiting the summits of Steel Fell, Calf Crag and saving the weird summit of Helm Crag for a thrilling finale.

Distance: 8 miles/13km	*fellwalking on fairly clear*
Height gain:	*paths, with care needed*
2,165ft/660m	*in mist.*
Walking time: 5 hours	*Start/Finish: Grasmere.*
Type of walk: Moderate	GR337076.

This walk leaves Grasmere via Easedale Road, which runs past Butharlyp Howe Youth Hostel, set in finely wooded grounds. There is a footpath running parallel to the road for a while, so that traffic can be avoided. Turn right at the next road junction to pass Thorny How Youth Hostel and continue along the road until it descends gently towards a bridge. Don't cross the bridge, but turn left along another minor road and cross another bridge near the hamlet of Town Head.

Turn left up a driveway which is signposted as "footpath only", and follow it uphill to reach a white building. Go through a gate on the left and turn immediately right to start following a grassy path running uphill through bracken. There are two more gates to go through at the start of this climb up on to Steel Fell, then the path climbs more steeply up a blunt ridge. There are two knuckles of rock protruding from the ridge which deflect the path right each time. Later, the gradient eases and the summit cairn lies just beyond at 1,811ft/552m.

To leave the summit of Steel Fell, keep left and follow a fence along the hummocky crest of the fell. When this fence turns sharply right, leave it and follow instead the sparse remains of an older fence, of which little remains but occasional iron posts aligned along the boggy, rocky, hummocky crest. There is generally a trodden path within sight of these old posts which passes a prominent little pool of water on the broad crest. The path and posts then lead towards the rather shapeless mass of Calf Crag, where a short climb uphill leads to the summit cairn at 1,762ft/537m.

In mist this point could be reached without any great trouble, but in poor visibility care is needed descending from Calf Crag. There is a path along the rugged, hummocky ridge leading towards Gibson Knott and Helm Crag. This is a switchback ridge and features a host of rocky little tops with a series of little gaps between them. It is possible in this sort of terrain to pass the summit of Gibson Knott without even realising.

There is a more significant gap on the ridge just before the final climb on to Helm Crag. This notch should be unmistakeable, as the ground beyond it suddenly rears up steeply. A short, steep and rocky climb leads on to an amazing summit ridge.

Here, at close quarters, are the weirdly-shaped rocky excrescences first noticed from the road far below. With diligence it is possible to work out how this chaotic mass of shattered stone forms the distinctive profiles seen from afar. The Howitzer is instantly recognisable – a tilted tower of rock pointing as if to fire a shot across towards Fairfield. The summit of Helm Crag is generally given as

1,299ft/396m, but this monolith is obviously the highest point.

An ascent of The Howitzer is optional. It can be done by gingerly picking a way up its back. Climbers will have little trouble with it, but walkers may decide against it.

Proceed further along the rocky crest and start the descent, where a fine view opens up across the lovely Vale of Grasmere. A short stretch of fencing steers walkers off to the right. The way down to Grasmere was once so horribly eroded that it had to be completely closed to walkers. Another path was constructed and this must be followed faithfully. It was pitched in stone, with zigzags to ease the gradient, and leads downhill more quickly, conveniently and safely than any other route. There are some old quarries to study on the lower wooded slopes.

At the bottom of the path, go through a large gate, and immediately turn left through a smaller gate. This gate leads on to a permitted path, running through pleasant woodlands to emerge in front of Lancrigg, where teas may be enjoyed. Leave Lancrigg by following the access road away from the house and back into woods. On reaching a minor road, Easedale Road, turn left and follow it back towards Grasmere. The village has interesting galleries, gift shops, and Wordsworth associations aplenty.

THIRLMERE

Thirlmere does not look like other lakes in this book. Its flanking hillsides are too steep and it often features an ugly, sterile rim whenever the water level falls. Thirlmere is not really a lake at all, but a reservoir serving distant Manchester. Before it became a reservoir it was two smaller lakes and its setting was quite different. There were a couple of farming hamlets, fields and fellsides, with only a few woods and trees. The farms and fields have been submerged, and the fellsides planted with alien conifers. From the point of construction, access to the area was banned by the waterworks authorities, but the ban has been relaxed by degrees and there is now a high level of access for visitors.

Two walks are offered from the shores of Thirlmere. One walk makes a complete circuit around the reservoir, sticking close to the shore on

Watendlath

Stanley Bond

the western side, but climbing to a higher level to pass around the eastern side. The route is mostly forested, but there are some clear spaces, plenty of good tracks and paths, and some quite good views.

The other walk takes in part of the Thirlmere shore, then climbs over a boggy crest to chart a course for the lovely hamlet of Watendlath. A descent to Watendlath for tea is an optional extra, before the route crosses back over the fells to return to Thirlmere.

Facilities on both these walks are very limited. There are only a couple of places offering food or drink, but short diversions need to be made to reach them. Buses pass back and forth on the main road, leading quickly to Keswick and Grasmere. Accommodation options are all off route and include a campsite, Youth Hostel, B&B and hotel accommodation.

This book covers walks in the western half of the Lake District, with the dividing line passing Thirlmere. A companion volume covers another 35 walks in the eastern half, taking in the Helvellyn range which rises from the shores of Thirlmere.

34 Thirlmere

Leatheswater and Brackmere are names which are unfamiliar to Lakeland visitors. Scour the map in vain for them. It's not a detailed map which is required, but an old one! The two lakes were identified in 1868 as having the potential to slake the growing thirst of Manchester and in the 1890s the two lakes were converted into one large reservoir, called Thirlmere. At first, access to the lake was forbidden, but times have changed and there is now a lengthy permitted shoreline path which can be linked with forest tracks to form a complete circuit.

Distance:
10 miles/16km
Height gain:
490ft/150m
Walking time: 6 hours
Type of walk: Along roads, tracks and paths beside the shore or through forests.
Start/Finish: The Swirls car park, near Thirlspot. GR316169.

The Swirls car park is situated between the forest and the open fell not far from Thirlspot. Many people who park there have their sights fixed on Helvellyn. The walk around Thirlmere is essentially low-level.

Leave the car park and cross the main road, then follow a path down through fields to reach the wooded shores of Thirlmere. Turn right to follow the path through the woods, and note that the path is often a good step away from the shoreline.

Dalehead Hall is largely out of sight, but is passed quite closely.

The rugged, wooded hill of Great How rises ahead, and by keeping to the left the path cuts around its base. Steps lead down on to a minor road and a left turn leads straight on to the monumental stone dam of the reservoir. A huge tablet inscribed with the names of Manchester Waterworks Committee members adorns a recess in the parapet of the dam. Continue across the dam and follow the minor road onwards. When a junction with another road is reached, drop to a wooded strip between the road and the shore of Thirlmere. The path can be vague, but is so narrow it is impossible to get lost.

There are a couple of car parks beside the shore of Thirlmere, and these make useful reference points. The car park at Armboth appears first. Old maps show a small settlement at Armboth, where a footbridge spanned the narrows between the two former lakes of Leatheswater and Brackmere.

The wooded shoreline path continues, and there are two wooded islands which will be noticed in the reservoir, Deergarth How Island and Hawes How Island. Formerly, these were hills, and when the lake level is low other little drowned hills appear as stony islands. Launchy Gill, a beck which features fine waterfalls in its upper reaches, spills into the reservoir between the two islands. When the path approaches Hause Point, the road must be joined, as a steep rockface falls straight into the water. There is a viewing point on top of Hause Point and this is worth visiting.

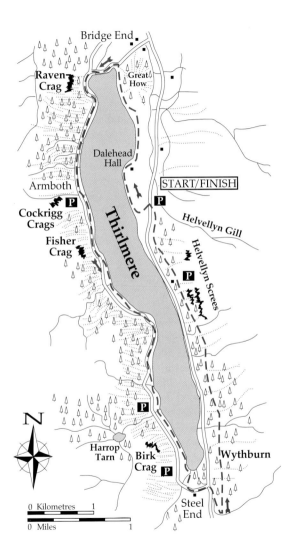

Bridge End

Raven
Crag

Great
How

Dalehead
Hall

START/FINISH

Armboth

Helvellyn Gill

Cockrigg
Crags

Fisher
Crag

Helvellyn Screes

Thirlmere

N

Harrop
Tarn

Birk
Crag

Wythburn

Steel
End

0 Kilometres 1

0 Miles 1

The road passes Hause Point and the shoreline path can be joined again immediately. Another car park is reached beside Dob Gill, where a walk up alongside the river would reveal waterfalls, but these are off route. Before the reservoir was formed, there was a cluster of farm buildings below Dob Gill known as The City. Continuing towards the head of Thirlmere, the wooded strip between the shore and the road is rather wider, so walkers will be less aware of traffic. The minor road is joined at a point where Wyth Burn flows beneath Stackhow Bridge, and a left turn needs to be made to approach the main A591 road nearby.

Cross the road and pick up a forest track heading off to the right, which gradually climbs above the level of the road. Keep turning left as the edge of the forest is gained, so that in effect the route turns back on itself. A forest track can then be followed which contours across the steep slopes above Wythburn Church, high above Thirlmere and away from the main road.

There are a couple of breaks in the forest plantations where vigorous becks cascade down steep slopes from Helvellyn. Footbridges lead walkers across and maintain dry feet. The forest track dwindles until it is merely a path between the trees, but it remains clearly trodden and is unlikely to be lost. In any case, the way becomes much broader as the car park at The Swirls is approached on the final descent at the end of the walk.

35 Watendlath

The lovely hamlet of Watendlath is usually thought of as a place which is approached from Borrowdale. While most visitors do come from that direction, walkers can arrive from almost any direction and a number of popular paths converge there. For a complete change, this route reaches Watendlath from Armboth, on the shores of Thirlmere. It starts with a walk alongside Thirlmere, then involves two high moorland crossings, with Watendlath situated in between. If the teashop at Watendlath is open, it will doubtless prove irresistible.

Distance:
8 miles/13km
Height gain:
1,970ft/600m
Walking time: 5 hours
Type of walk: Lakeshore, forest and moorland walking, with some paths being vague.
Start/Finish: Armboth, beside Thirlmere. GR305172.

The car park at Armboth is located on a forested stretch of the Thirlmere shore. There is nothing at Armboth apart from the car park, but there was once a settlement which was drowned during the construction of the reservoir in the 1890s.

There is a path leaving Armboth which runs southwards along the wooded strip in between the minor road and the reservoir shore. This runs past the wooded islands of Deergarth How Island and

Hawse How Island. It is necessary to come up on to the minor road to pass Hause Point, as a rockface drops sheer into the water. There is a viewpoint on top of the rock which is worth the short climb. The shoreline path continues southwards from Hause Point to a car park at Dob Gill.

Cross the minor road at Dob Gill and follow a path uphill from the car park. This climbs steeply up the forested slope to pass the hidden pool of Harrop Tarn. Turn right to follow a track, then look out for a small sign which indicates the way to Watendlath on the left. Later, branch to the right and look carefully for occasional bridleway arrows and cairns which show the way onwards to the edge of the forest. The bridleway leaves the forest and proceeds rather vaguely over the higher moors beyond. As height is gained, look ahead to spot a gate in a fence on the broad moorland crest.

Go through the gate and follow a boggy path onwards, which runs fairly close to Blea Tarn in a lonely moorland hollow. There are fine views across to Borrowdale. Take care to climb slightly after passing Blea Tarn and don't follow Bleatarn Gill downstream. Follow a sparsely cairned path across the boggy moorland, looking ahead to spot a wall and then follow it roughly northwards.

There are striking bird's-eye views down towards Watendlath, which nestles in a hollow occupied by a number of fields and the bright mirror of Watendlath Tarn.

A zigzag path leads down to Watendlath if

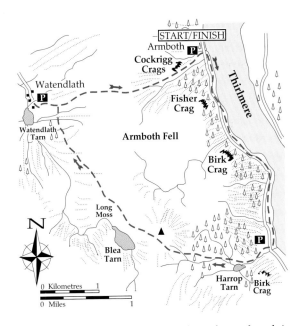

explorations are to be conducted, or if a tea break is required. This was once a Norse settlement, which later became a property of Furness Abbey. It has also featured in Hugh Walpole's *Herries* novels and the home of Judith Paris is adorned with a plaque. After having a look around, and feeding the ducks and chaffinches with scraps of food, follow the zigzag path back uphill.

There is a small stand of trees at the top of the initial steep climb, where a small sign confirms that this is the way over to Armboth. The path used to leave Armboth is quite clear, being pitched in stone, but its continuation becomes rather vague on the higher moors. There is a gate in a fence which crosses the boggy summit of High Tove at 1,665ft/515m.

This is the last place from which to sample a decent view before the descent. The fells closest to the summit block any decent views to north or south, but the westward prospects embrace the Grasmoor and Buttermere Fells, proceeding past Great Gable and Scafell Pike, to Bow Fell and Crinkle Crags. Eastwards, the flank of the Helvellyn range dominates, and will be seen practically all the way downhill to the end of the walk.

Take greater care following the path down from High Tove in mist. It crosses boggy, heathery ground and can be difficult to trace in places. The ground steepens and there is a sudden drop into the little valley drained by Fisher Gill. A zigzag path leads down into the valley, and there are steep and rugged slopes off to the left called Cockrigg Crags. The other side of the little valley is forested and the path simply follows the forest fence downhill. The minor road which runs along the length of Thirlmere is joined, and by crossing it walkers are led straight back to the car park at Armboth.

FURTHER READING

Lakeland Villages, Jim Watson, (Cicerone Press).

Lakeland Towns, Jim Watson, (Cicerone Press).

Coniston Coppermines, Eric Holland, (Cicerone Press).

A Dream of Eden, John Dawson, (Cicerone Press).

Companion Guide to the Lake District, Frank Welsh, (Collins).

The Lakeland Peaks, Walter Poucher, (Constable).

Lake District Landscape Heritage, William Rollinson (ed), (David & Charles).

50 Best Scrambles in the Lake District, Bill O'Connor, (David & Charles).

The Naturalist in Lakeland, Eric Hardy, (David & Charles).

A Pictorial Guide to the Lakeland Fells – North Western, Western, Southern & Central Fells, A Wainwright, (Michael Joseph).

The Outlying Fells of Lakeland, A Wainwright, (Michael Joseph).

The Lakers, Norman Nicholson, (Robert Hale).

Other Dalesman titles for walkers

Walking and Trail Guides
Lake District Western Fells Paddy Dillon £4.99
Yorkshire Dales North & East Terry Marsh £4.99
Yorkshire Dales South & West Terry Marsh £4.99

Walks Around Series: Yorkshire
Grassington Richard Musgrave £1.99
Hawes Richard Musgrave £1.99
Helmsley Nick Channer £1.99
Kirkbymoorside Nick Channer £1.99
Pickering Nick Channer £1.99
Richmond Richard Musgrave £1.99
Settle & Malham Richard Musgrave £1.99
Whitby Nick Channer £1.99

Walks Around Series: Lake District
Ambleside Tom Bowker £1.99
Coniston & Hawkshead Mary Welsh £1.99
Keswick Dawn Gibson £1.99
Windermere Robert Gambles £1.99

Pub Walks Series
Lancashire Terry Marsh £5.99
Lake District Terry Marsh £5.99
Peak District John Morrison £5.99
North York Moors & Coast Richard Musgrave £5.99

Tea Shop Walks Series
Lake District Mary Welsh £5.99
Yorkshire Dales Richard Musgrave £5.99
North York Moors & Coast Mark Reid £5.99

Walker's Guide Series
Three Peaks & Malhamdale W R Mitchell £6.95
Cleveland Hills Tom Scott Burns £6.95

Long-Distance Walks
Cumbria Way John Trevelyan £2.99
Dales Way Colin Speakman £2.99

Safety for Walkers
Map Reading Robert Matkin £3.50

Available from all good bookshops.
In case of difficulty, or for a list of Dalesman titles, contact:
Dalesman Publishing
The Water Mill, Broughton Hall,
Skipton, North Yorkshire BD23 3AG.
Tel: (+44) 01756 701033   Website: www.dalesman.co.uk